RECAPTURING

the

GLORY

of

CHRISTMAS

R. Albert Mohler Jr.

RECAPTURING

the

GLORY

of

CHRISTMAS

A 25-Day Advent Devotional

PUBLISHING®
BRENTWOOD, TENNESSEE

978-1-4300-9731-0

Published by B&H Publishing Group
Brentwood, Tennessee

Dewey Decimal Classification: 263.91
Subject Heading: JESUS CHRIST—NATIVITY
/ CHRISTMAS / ADVENT

2 3 4 5 6 7 · 28 27 26 25 24

To my wonderful Mary,
with whom I have shared more than
forty sweet Christmases, and our son Christopher,
and to our daughter, Katie, now with her husband Riley
and
their precious children Benjamin, Henry, and Mary
Margaret,
with whom every celebration of the birth of Christ
is so joyous and wonderful.
Thank you for making every day of my life so sweet.

And to Ann Mohler, my sweet Aunt Ann, the last of
that great generation in my family who surrounded
me with love and remains so incredibly
encouraging and faithful.

From the depth of my heart
Merry Christmas

Acknowledgments

Honestly, no author works alone. I owe a debt to churches like Southside Baptist Church in Lakeland, Florida, and First Baptist Church, Pompano Beach, Florida, for gospel preaching and for exulting in Christ in the celebration of Christmas when I was a child and teenager. I am just as thankful for my late parents, Dick and Janet Mohler, for their commitment to Christ and the celebration of Christmas in our home. Then, at an even deeper level, I turn to my cherished wife Mary, and to our children, Katie and Christopher, and the memories of our Christmases together. Now, our Christmas joy is greatly amplified by celebration that includes Katie's husband, Riley Barnes, and three precious grandchildren, Benjamin, Henry, and Margaret. We teach each other Christmas and exult in the light of the incarnation of Christ.

In my office, I am particularly thankful for Caleb Shaw, chief of staff, Graham Faulkner, director of communications, Nick Mottola, digital content coordinator, and Cory Higdon, who served as director of presidential research. I am also thankful for a team of interns who worked with me at this time, including Carlo Cicero, Ben Pinkston,

Alex Richey, William Wolfe, Jacob Page, Christopher Parr, Austin Puckett, J. P. Shafer, Caleb Green, and Marc Cogan. Anna Arrastia and Allison Moldenhauer keep the trains running on time, efficiently and so graciously.

Contents

Contents

Recapturing the Glory of Christmas

Christmas comes year after year. Even in our secularized, post-Christian culture, our society cannot escape Christmas. This season only exists because God in Christ came into the world to save sinners. Yet believers and nonbelievers alike celebrate it every year, spending enormous amounts of time, money, and energy on one day in the month of December. If you drive down your neighborhood street on a December night, you will likely find numerous homes decorated with lights and sparkling trees displayed in front of windows. But how many of your neighbors understand what they celebrate? We are told "Merry Christmas" as we bustle about from store to store, but does the barista or checkout clerk grasp the meaning of the word *Christmas* and why we should be merry about it? Even more perplexing is this: How many *Christians* comprehend the incalculable glory of this season?

Our secularized society can subtly coax Christians away from biblical fidelity on any number of issues. Indeed, the apostle Paul's command and warning in Romans 12:2 shows how easily surrounding customs—even pagan ones—could derail Christian commitment to God: "Do not be conformed to this age," he wrote, "but be transformed by the renewing of your mind, so that you may discern what is the good, pleasing, and perfect will of God." Christians, in other words, will conform their hearts and minds toward either godliness or ungodliness, and this includes a danger that we let the Christmas season pass us by without seeing and savoring the truths God has revealed to us.

The modern age is seductive, and even Christians are tempted to miss the imperishable glory of Christmas as we celebrate the birth of our own Savior. In short, our culture has scandalized Christmas. Materialism has replaced the Messiah, and Santa has eclipsed the Savior. Perfectly wrapped presents placed under evergreens rob the affections of men and women, young and old, from something far more spectacular and joyful. We have commercialized Christmas, and Christians can, lamentably, capitulate to the downward spiral of confusion that distorts the Christmas message.

The Bible, however, leaves no room for confusion. God's infallible, inerrant Word will not allow us to trade the glory of the incomparable God for the glory of created things. Indeed, regarding Christmas, the Scriptures summon the world to come and behold a wonderous, glorious display of God's immeasurable love for the world. God revealed in his Word the Advent of his beloved Son—the incarnation of God in Christ who had come to dwell among us. This Immanuel, "God with us" (Matt. 1:23 ESV), broke into a sinful world—lost in dark depravity—that he might cast the saving light of redemption. This is the glory of Christmas.

The prophet Isaiah wrote, "The people walking in darkness have seen a great light; a light has dawned on those living in the land of darkness" (Isa. 9:2). Christmas reminds us that light has come and the darkness has been overcome. Those words from Isaiah declare the coming Prince of Peace and the light and life he would bring. Indeed, the Savior has come. Christmas marks the Advent of God's only Son, who would come to dispel the darkness, put death to death, and secure everlasting life for the people of God. Christmas, then, marks not only the birth of Jesus in Bethlehem as a fulfillment of biblical prophecy but the dawn of a new age. Christmas is far more than a season of sleigh bells and smiling children. It is the crux of all history. It is the inbreaking of the light into darkness. It is the birth of the Lord and Savior of the world. History is cut in two, and sinners are redeemed by the blood of the Lamb.

Light has always been central to the Christmas season. Families string lights around trees, and fathers bravely ascend ladders to string lights around the perimeter of the house, illuminating their homes with displays of brilliance and color. The warm glow of lighted candles dispels the darkness. Christmas bears a sense of radiance as a season of light. While the lights of the modern Christmas season might serve as mere decoration, the prophet Isaiah understood light as a mark of divine revelation. The light of Christmas represents God's glorious revelation, when a young woman named Mary gave birth to the Light of the world.

Indeed, in John's Gospel, the apostle spoke of Jesus Christ as the true light from God which would enlighten every man. John declared, "In him was life, and that life was the light of men. The light shines in the darkness, and yet the darkness did not overcome it" (John 1:4–5). The birth of Jesus Christ brought the unconquerable light of divine majesty. When the eternal Son of God humbled himself by taking the form of a servant, he came with a salvific light that lifted the veil of the kingdom of darkness.

The need of this Light points to the harrowing reality of the darkness. All humanity lives under the black shadow of sin and shame. The darkness which blanketed the world inhibited everyone from seeing and knowing God. Darkness befell the creation all the way back in Genesis 3 when Adam and Eve, through a display of high treason, disobeyed God and subsequently plunged the creation and the cosmos under the shadow of sin. God, however, promised a day of redemption. Indeed, in Genesis 3, God cursed the serpent, pronouncing, "I will put hostility between you and the woman, and between your offspring and her offspring. He will strike your head, and you will strike his heel" (Gen. 3:15). From that day forward, God continually spoke of a day when the curse would be reversed, when the light would break through the darkness, when redemption would rescue people from their sin.

That is what happened at Jesus's birth. The birth of Christ marked the culmination of all God's promises. God incarnate had come as "the true light that gives light to everyone" (John 1:9). *This* marks the glory of Christmas.

Our culture has surrendered the everlasting Light and incarnation for a Christmas season emptied of the radiance of the glory of God; and if we are not careful, Christians can forget Paul's instructions and let ourselves be conformed to this world. It is incumbent on God's people to hasten toward repentance, to recapture the splendor of this season, and to reinvigorate our affections with the glorious truths of Advent. The refrain of that Christian hymn, "O Come Let Us Adore Him," should serve as the anthem for all believers in this season. God, by his grace, has cast his glorious light and saved his people from the darkness of their sin. The veil is lifted; the darkness has receded because the Light has come.

Christmas means worship and adoration, and I intend this Advent devotional as a call to worship and praise. Each day will mine the depths of the Bible and its teachings about Advent and Christmas. We will dwell on all the theological riches God has gifted to his people through Christmas. Indeed, Christmas beckons the world to come and adore the Savior King: the King exulted by the angels; the King who took on flesh; the King who deserves *all* glory, *all* honor, and *all* praise.

O come let us adore him, Christ, the Lord.

Where Does the Christmas Story Begin?

The Word became flesh and dwelt
among us. We observed his glory, the
glory as the one and only Son from
the Father, full of grace and truth.

John 1:14

As the celebration of Christmas fast approaches, our attention quickly goes to the familiar words of the infancy narratives found in the Gospels of Matthew and Luke. This is a healthy reflex. After all, the gospel of Jesus Christ rests upon the historicity of the events that took place in Bethlehem more than two thousand years ago. Our understanding of the identity of Jesus Christ is directly rooted in these biblical narratives, and our confidence is in the fact that Matthew and Luke give us historically credible and completely truthful accounts of the events surrounding the birth of Jesus.

A closer look at the narratives in both Matthew and Luke reveals a richness that familiarity may hide from us. Matthew begins with the genealogy of Christ, demonstrating the sequence of generations as Israel anticipated the birth of David's Son, the Messiah. Luke, intending to set forth "an orderly sequence" (1:3) of the events concerning Jesus, begins with the anticipation of the birth of John the Baptist and then moves on to tell of the virgin conception of Jesus.

A careful reading of Matthew and Luke shows both the elegance of detail and the grand expanse of the story of Christ's birth. Matthew gives particular attention to the fulfillment of Old Testament prophecy. The virgin birth, the birth of Christ in Bethlehem of Judea, the Herodian massacre of the innocents, the flight to Egypt, and the role of John the Baptist as forerunner are all presented as the fulfillment of specific Old Testament prophecies.

Every word of the Old Testament points to Christ. He is not only the fulfillment of all the Old Testament prophecies concerning him; he is the perfect fulfillment of the Law and the Prophets—the entirety of the Old Testament Scriptures. The Christmas story does not begin in Bethlehem, for Israel had been promised the Messiah even before then. As Luke reveals, Simeon beheld the baby Jesus in the temple and understood this infant to be "the Lord's Christ" (ESV)—the Davidic Messiah (Luke 2:25–32). Simeon understood this clearly: the Christmas story did not begin in Bethlehem, or even in Jerusalem; it began as the eternal purposes of God, even before the world was created.

Where, then, *does* the Christmas story begin? In the Gospel of John we read: "In the beginning was the Word, and the Word was with God, and the Word was God. He was with God in the beginning. All things were created through him, and apart from him not one thing was created that has been created" (John 1:1–3).

The prologue to John's Gospel points to creation and to Christ, the divine Logos, and the agent of creation. Yet, with language drawn directly from Genesis, John begins his Gospel, "In the beginning."

In other words, the Christmas story begins *before the creation of the world*. As we celebrate Christmas and contemplate the Christmas story, we must be careful not to begin the story in Bethlehem, or even in Nazareth, where Mary was confronted by Gabriel with the message that she would be the mother of the Messiah.

We must not even begin with Moses and the prophets, and with the expectation of the coming Son of Man, the promised Suffering Servant, and the heralded Davidic Messiah. We must begin before the world was created and before humanity was formed, much less fallen.

Why is this so important? Put simply, if we get the "when" of the Christmas story wrong, we can affirm things about God and his will that are not true. Told carelessly, the Christmas story sounds like God's "Plan B." In other words, we can make the Christmas story sound like God turning to a new plan, rather than fulfilling all he had already promised. We must be careful to tell the Christmas story in such a way that we make the gospel clear.

Christmas is not God's second plan. Before he created the world, God determined to save sinners through the blood of his own Son. The grand narrative of the Bible points to this essential truth: God determined to bring glory to himself through the salvation of a people redeemed and purchased by his own Son, the Christ. Bethlehem and Calvary were essential parts of God's plan from the beginning, before the cosmos was brought into being.

The Christmas story does not begin in Bethlehem, but we appropriately look to Bethlehem as the scene of the most decisive event in human history—the incarnation of the Son of God. Even as we turn our attention to Bethlehem, we must remember that the story of our salvation does not begin there. That story begins in the eternal purpose of God.

"In the beginning was the Word, and the Word was with God, and the Word was God. He was with God in the beginning" (John 1:1). That is where the Christmas story begins, and John takes us right to the essence of what happened in

Bethlehem: "The Word became flesh and dwelt among us. We observed his glory, the glory as the one and only Son from the Father, full of grace and truth" (John 1:14).

Let's be sure to get the Christmas story right, start to finish.

3

A Properly Sentimental Season

"My soul magnifies the Lord, and
my spirit rejoices in God my Savior,
because he has looked with favor on
the humble condition of his servant."

Luke 1:46–48

Christmas is undoubtedly a time of joy and thanksgiving, a time with family and friends. Indeed, it is a time filled with worship as we remember that glorious gospel truth: "The Word became flesh and dwelt among us. We observed his glory, the glory as the one and only Son from the Father, full of grace and truth" (John 1:14).

But let's be honest. Christians often fail to recognize the sweetness of Christmas. Consider, for example, the interaction between Elizabeth and Mary at the beginning of Luke's Gospel. Their exchange provides a helpful pattern for Christian affections during this season, which, if we are not careful, can quickly devolve into a hectic holiday. When Elizabeth realized that Mary would give birth to the Messiah, she worshipped and declared sweet truths about God, his grace, and the coming of the promised Son of Man. Mary, too, marveled at the mercy of the Lord, with her Magnificat serving as a song of praise. She understood that the baby growing in her womb was a sweet and exceedingly glorious event that led her to declare, "My soul magnifies the Lord, and my spirit rejoices in God my Savior" (Luke 1:46–47).

The sweetness of this season, however, can be easily diminished by the temptations of busyness and material-ism; the commercialization of Christmas has secularized the story of Christ's birth. Christians must realize how easily we can jettison the sweetness of Christmas and let the glory of this season be eclipsed by this secular world.

Indeed, at this time of year, competing sentimen-talities vie for our affections. There is the sentimentality of a secularized Christmas, one that seeks happiness in the material goods of the season. We can lose ourselves in presents, food, or the music we only hear in the month of December. There is, however, another kind of sentimen-tality—a deep and authentic sentimentality of the Christian faith and the Christian gospel. That sentimentality is essential to our understanding of God's love for us. That sentimentality is necessary for Christmas.

Martin Luther was one figure in the history of the church who powerfully understood the glory and sweetness of Christmas. In fact, he understood sentiment as necessary, for it was revealed in the nativity stories contained in Matthew and Luke. There was a tenderness, a sweetness, between Mary and Elizabeth and between Mary and Joseph. There was a sweetness in the heart of Mary as she responded to the angel Gabriel's message with submission and obedience. There is a beauty in the lowly nature of Jesus's birth—the second person of the Trinity, the Son of God, the eternal Logos lying swaddled in a manger.

Luther wanted Christians to see this sweet narrative of God's inestimable love. The One who spoke the world into being became the baby in Bethlehem's manger. He condescended, in unimaginable humility, to become the son of Mary. He did not come into the world with the grandeur given to worldly princes and princesses. The Alpha and the Omega, the beginning and the end, the One who is the same yesterday, today, and forever was that tiny infant held in his mother's arms. This was the Savior of the world, the Lord Jesus Christ. He had come to rescue us from our sin.

To capture this sweetness, Martin Luther wrote a song for his own children at Christmas. The song concludes with these words:

This is the Christ, our God and Lord,
who in all need shall aid afford;
he will himself your Savior be from
all your sins to set you free.

These are the tokens ye shall mark:
the swadling clothes and manger dark;
there ye shall find the infant lady by whom
the heav'ns and earth were made.[1]

May you celebrate Christmas in all of its wonder, in all of its glory, in all of its grandeur—yes, in all of its sweetness. May you be filled with the knowledge of the glory of Christ, and may you proclaim that Christ has indeed come. Tell the whole story of Christ this season, from grandeur to sweetness. Teach it to your children and your grandchildren. Sing Christmas carols and sing them with gusto.

Celebrate the true sentiment of Christmas. Don't miss the glory, the sweetness, of Christmas.

4

On Them Has Light Shined

*The people who walked in darkness have
seen a great light; those who dwelt in a land
of deep darkness, on them has light shone.*

Isaiah 9:2 ESV

On July 15, 1838, Ralph Waldo Emerson delivered the commencement address for the graduates of Harvard Divinity School. Emerson was no orthodox Christian, and by this point Harvard's Divinity School had succumbed to the pressures of Protestant liberalism and accepted Unitarian theology. You can already guess what kind of address this would have been.

The most famous passage from Emerson's "Divinity School Address" included these words: "Let me admonish you, first of all, *to go it alone*; to refuse the good models, even those which are sacred in the imagination of men, and dare to love God without mediator or veil" (emphasis added).[2] He

17

went on to argue that those in Christian ministry should cast off all tradition and conformity to eighteen centuries of Christian theology. He sought a theological independence from every authority and model, including the Bible, the prophets, and the apostles.

That kind of sentiment has only burgeoned since Emerson gave his address, with subjectivism and individualism becoming celebrated virtues in our culture. The tendency to follow Emerson's summons for a Christianity and ministry devoid of indebtedness and humility, however, runs contrary to the gospel and contrary to the season we celebrate as Christmas. Christians dare not "go it alone." We dare not approach God without the mediatory role of Christ our Savior. We cannot even hope to know God apart from his revelation to us and the deposit of the gospel he instilled in his church since the age of the apostles.

In other words, the Christian gospel—and what we celebrate at Christmas—refutes Emerson's mentality and rejects the prevailing worldview of our society. We have no hope in ourselves; that is why Christ had to come.

Indeed, consider the words of the prophet Isaiah: "The people who walked in darkness have seen a great light; those who dwelt in a land of deep darkness, on them has light shone" (Isa. 9:2 ESV). The light shone *on* them; they did not seek the light, find the light, or devise the light. The light shone on them.

The picture revealed in this passage is easy to understand, but it is so profound that it frames our entire understanding of the incarnation and the essence of the gospel. Under the curse of sin, we fumble about in the darkness. But, as Isaiah prophesied, a light would come, shining on God's people and bringing them out of the pit of despair.

This light is nothing less than a picture of God's revelation. He has revealed his truth to us. He has cast his marvelous light. Light broke into the world. Christ's incarnation pierced the darkness and depravity of our state. Christmas, then, is the declaration that God is there, he is not silent, and he has come to rescue his people. Christmas is a brilliant remembrance of the grace and mercy of God.

Contrary to Emerson and the individualism of our age, Christmas humbles us. Indeed, Isaiah's prophecy, quoted in Matthew and Luke (Matt. 4:15–16; Luke 1:79), provides us a portrait of grace and the sheer unmerited favor of God. We do not deserve the light, but it has shone on us, and we have seen the great light of Jesus Christ.

Light is a powerful metaphor for revelation, understanding, and salvation. It resounds throughout the Bible's own disclosure of the gospel and its promises. In fact, light is a category in nearly every major religious system, but the way it is used in biblical Christianity has a crucial distinction. There are those who look for the light within, but the Bible is clear: we depend on the light from without. We are not to look within ourselves for the light. Left to our own devices, to the ethic of "going it alone,"[3] we would remain perennially lost in darkness and shame. We do not look for hope *in* us. We look for the light that has come *to* us, a light that has come to transform us from one degree of glory to another.

Emerson's way leads to theological disaster and the abandonment of the gospel. It will rob Christmas of the joy we celebrate this season—a joy that exists only because "the true light that gives light to everyone was coming into the world" (John 1:9). And "to all who did receive him, he gave them the right to be children of God, to those who believe in his name" (John 1:12).

A lesser-known Christmas hymn written by W. Chatterton Dix, "As with Gladness Men of Old," captures this beauty of the light of Christmas and the grace it provides for those who will follow Jesus:

> As with gladness men of old
> did the guiding star behold;
> as with joy they hailed its light,
> leading onward, beaming bright;
> so, most gracious God, may we
> evermore be led to Thee.
>
> As with joyful steps they sped,
> to that lowly cradle-bed,

there to bend the knee before
Him whom heav'n and earth adore;
so may we with willing feet
ever seek Thy mercy-seat.

Holy Jesus, ev'ry day
keep us in the narrow way;
and, when earthly things are past,
bring our ransomed souls at last
where they need no star to guide,
where no clouds Thy glory hide.

In that heav'nly country bright
need they no created light;
Thou its Light, its Joy, its Crown,
Thou its Sun which goes not down;
there for ever may we sing
alleluias to our King.[4]

Christians, the Light of the world has come. He has
shone on you and brought you out of *your* darkness and *your*
sin. This Christmas, celebrate this wonderous declaration
and rest in the exceeding grace of God for *you*.

Our Great High Priest

For Christ did not enter a sanctuary made
with hands (only a model of the true one)
but into heaven itself, so that he might
now appear in the presence of God for us.
Hebrews 9:24

Trials, suffering, pain, and temptation mark the road to the heavenly city. The promises of future glory, though spectacular, mean little if Christians must endure this life alone. That is especially true of a life that means living sinlessly in a sinful world, against the threatening schemes of Satan and the weaknesses of the flesh. The incarnation, however, points not only to future faithfulness and promises but to how we can face present trials. How? Because by becoming like us, by taking on flesh, the Son of God became our great high priest.

Hebrews 2:17 states, "Therefore, he had to be like his brothers and sisters in every way, so that he could become a merciful and faithful high priest in matters pertaining to God, to make atonement for the sins of the people." The Christmas season calls Christians to worship the God who took on flesh, showing to the world the incalculable mercy of God in Christ. God looked upon us, sinners though we are, and there displaced his infinite mercy. He did not wipe us out. He sent his beloved Son that he might be our brother, secure everlasting hope, then propitiate for our sins, and intercede for us as our high priest.

Under the old covenant, the priests represented the nation of Israel. The priestly class mediated between God and the people. Once a year, the high priest would enter the holy of holies on Yom Kippur, the Day of Atonement. Once in the most sacred place, the high priest would make the sacrifice on behalf of himself and the people. Because he had to make a sacrifice for his own sins, he provided a limited mediation. He could not stand before God as a perfect mediator between God and the people. He, too, needed forgiveness.

The incarnation, however, inaugurated a new priesthood. Jesus Christ, the sinless one, assumed the priestly office and entered the holy of holies. He did not enter the physical place in the temple. In fact, the author of Hebrews declared, "For Christ did not enter a sanctuary made with hands (only a model of the true one) but into heaven itself,

so that he might now appear in the presence of God for us"
(Heb. 9:24). Jesus, therefore, passed through the true veil
of heaven. He did not enter a copy into the veiled presence
of God. He stood before the full presence of God. There,
in his perfection, he did something no priest in Israel's
history ever did: he laid down his own life as the spotless
sacrifice. Jesus Christ, therefore, because of his incarnation, could enter the holy of holies as God yet serve as man's
perfect priest and sacrifice for sin. The perfect high priest
performed the perfect sacrifice once for all.

Christians, this is the glory of Christmas. Why would
you trade the spectacular riches of God's mercy in Christ
for a Christmas season dominated by materialism and false
promises? This season declares that, through the incarnation, Jesus Christ assumed flesh and became the perfect
high priest for mankind. This truth should encourage us in
at least four ways:

First, mankind needs a mediator between us and God.
Christmas should be not only a season of great joy but also
a harrowing reminder of the cost of our sin. The ravages
of our rebellion bore such a penalty that God had to send
his only Son to save us. Only the perfect Son of God could
be our remedy. Our sin was so great that nothing on earth,
nothing in all the cosmos, could rectify our state. Only the
one Son of God and Man could mediate on our behalf.

Second, Jesus's role as high priest reveals the infinite love of God for his children. God could have satisfied his justice by executing judgment on all mankind. God, however, showered from the courts of heaven an inestimable grace, a pure redeeming love for his people. John 3:16 says, "For God loved the world in this way: He gave his one and only Son, so that everyone who believes in him will not perish but have eternal life." Romans 5:8 resounds, "But God proves his own love for us in that while we were still sinners, Christ died for us." Second Corinthians 5:21 declares, "He made the one who did not know sin to be sin for us, so that in him we might become the righteousness of God." First Peter 2:24 proclaims, "He himself bore our sins in his body on the tree; so that, having died to sins, we might life for righteousness. By his wounds you have been healed."

The God of the universe poured out his love on us by sending his Son. This is the story of amazing grace. God heard the cries of his enslaved people, held in chains by Egypt. He heard their cries and sent them a deliverer. In an infinitely more profound way, God the Son descended from his throne to become our deliverer. This is what we celebrate at Christmas.

Third, Jesus's ministry as high priest enables true worship and faithfulness. Jesus Christ set us free from sin by making full propitiation for our sins. This means he appeased the wrath of God in full. The power of forgiveness rings in

Romans where Paul declared, "What a wretched man I am!
Who will rescue me from this body of death? Thanks be to
God through Jesus Christ our Lord! . . . Therefore, there is
now no condemnation for those in Christ Jesus, because the
law of the Spirit of life in Christ Jesus has set you free from
the law of sin and death" (Rom. 7:24–25; 8:1–2). Christ, by
serving as our high priest, sets believers free from the law
of sin and death. Freedom reigns over the household of
faith—a freedom to know and obey God. Indeed, the freedom secured through Christ is a freedom to approach God
in boldness. We now worship God as his redeemed people,
saved by the blood of the Lamb.

*Fourth, by virtue of his incarnation, Christ serves as a
high priest who understands our weaknesses.* The author of
Hebrews reminds his readers, "For since [Jesus] himself
has suffered when he was tempted, he is able to help those
who are tempted" (Heb. 2:18). Christians announce at
Christmas that a high priest has come that draws us near
to God, who has suffered for us, who understands our
weaknesses and offers supernatural aid that enables his
people to endure this lifelong pilgrimage. Later the author
of Hebrews says, "For we do not have a high priest who is
unable to sympathize with our weaknesses, but one who
has been tempted in every way as we are, yet without sin"
(Heb. 4:15). Jesus, though sinless, was tempted, and thus
he understands our weaknesses. Indeed, in identifying

with us, Christ, though fully God, took on full humanity so that he might come to the aid of those who suffer and have come under the barrage of temptation. Only through the incarnation could we have this kind of high priest. Our great high priest *has* come, and thus we *are* saved. The baby in Bethlehem's manger is Christ Jesus the Lord, and that is the glory of Christmas.

Making All Things New

Now since the children have flesh and
blood in common, Jesus also shared
in these, so that through his death
he might destroy the one holding the
power of death—that is, the devil.

Hebrews 2:14

The Son of God took on flesh that he might make all things new. Through the incarnation, God revealed that the created world, which had succumbed to the curse of sin, would be made new and redeemed. The incarnation, therefore, marked a cosmic reversal of the curse of sin introduced in Genesis 3. The above Hebrews verse, furthermore, bears tremendous consequences and silences a heresy that would have been familiar to the original audience—indeed, a heresy that prevails in modern times. That heresy is Gnosticism.

Gnosticism derides the material world. It holds the physical world as irredeemably corrupt. All human beings, therefore, should liberate the mind from the body, gnostics teach. The body is a prison that must be escaped. This ancient heresy has gripped postmodern spirituality. Indeed, pop psychology and psychotherapy populate all the bookstores. Many think we can somehow, through mental exertion, will ourselves out of suffering, trials, and present circumstances.

The physical world must be escaped, according to the gnostics. Yet this kind of mental leap presupposes the purity of the mind—a mind the Bible presents as just as corrupt as the body. No amount of mental power will ever lead the mind from the corruption of the flesh because the mind itself remains enslaved to the ravages of sin and death.

The Bible teaches that true freedom flows from the full redemption secured by Jesus Christ. We are not disembodied spirits trying to escape a physical world. We are lost sinners who desperately need a Savior. Our celebration of Christmas commemorates that salvation. The Christmas message proclaims that the fullness of redemption has come. When the Son of God took on flesh, he came to enact a holistic salvation—a work that would free not only our minds from corruption but even our bodies. As the author of Hebrews noted, Jesus, by his death, brought an end to death. He raided the fortress of Satan and vanquished our ancient foe by taking from him the power he held over all of creation. In so doing, the ministry of Christ secured a redemption that has made and will make all things new.

While the promise of Jesus's coming to make all things new rejects Gnosticism, the mission of the incarnation also pushes us away from any mere materialism. The Christmas season can easily turn into a time to dwell on perishable gifts. Children are especially prone to the unceasing wave of advertisements that feature the latest toys and games. Any parent can testify to the noticeable uptick in the phrase "I want that!" from toddlers and young children during the Christmas season. Yet adults, too, can buy into the temptations of materialism that come during the Christmas season. In doing so, we forget that "our citizenship is in heaven, and we eagerly wait for a Savior from there, the Lord Jesus Christ" (Phil. 3:20). Christmas reorients our focus on the mission of Jesus to make all things new by his incarnation. It reminds us that this world will one day give way to the glorious inheritance that awaits all those who believed in Jesus—the eternal life he secured by being born in the manger.

When Jesus took on flesh, God declared that the creation he had made would be made new. The world he created—indeed, the bodies of believers—would not be obliterated but remade, refashioned in the new heavens and the new earth. Christmas, therefore, brings with it an eschatological—an end-time—hope for the world. The fear of death no longer holds power, nor can it enslave those who belong to Christ. Why? Because Christ has come. He was born in a manger for us. He lived for us. He died for us. He paid the eternal price of God's wrath for us. He came so that we might live forever. This, however, he could not do unless he became like us in every way.

Not only do we announce in this season the coming of the Savior, but we also proclaim a day when sin will be no more, when death will have no power, when Satan will forever be silent, and when all tears will be wiped away. Our Christmas carols ring with the message of the birth of the Son of God who dwelt among his people in the flesh, who radiated grace and light, and who secured through his ministry the city of heaven. As we celebrate Christmas, meditate on this particular aspect of *why* Jesus came. He came so that we might inherit the new Jerusalem, a new earth, where God will dwell with his people forever and ever. He came as the fulfillment of *all* God's promises.

The Fullness of God in Christ

For God was pleased to have all his fullness
dwell in him, and through him to reconcile
everything to himself, whether things on
earth or things in heaven, by making peace
through his blood, shed on the cross.
Colossians 1:19–20

Christmas marks the coming of the fullness of God in Christ. In Colossians 1:9–12, Paul summons the church to a true knowledge of God with eternal significance. Indeed, he reminds all Christians of the Father's overwhelming love for his children by making them heirs of an eternal inheritance.

Then, in verses 13–17, Paul writes,

> He has rescued us from the domain of
> darkness and transferred us into the

kingdom of the Son he loves. In him we
have redemption, the forgiveness of sins.

> He is the image of the invisible God,
> the firstborn over all creation.
> For everything was created by him,
> in heaven and on earth,
> the visible and the invisible,
> whether thrones or dominions
> or rulers or authorities—
> all things have been created through him
> and for him.
> He is before all things,
> and by him all things hold together.

This is not a typical Christmas passage. I doubt many
pastors will look to Colossians 1:13–17 as the text for their
Christmas sermon. This passage, however, affirms a vital
doctrinal truth when it comes to Christmas—a truth without which there would be no good news to celebrate every
December. This passage proclaims the *full* deity of Jesus
Christ. Indeed, his divine nature explains the glorious
splendor of God the Son. Jesus is the one who made all things
by the power of his word, and he upholds the universe by his
grace. Furthermore, Paul reveals in verses 19–20 that at the
incarnation "all the fullness of God was pleased to dwell, and
through him to reconcile to himself all things, whether on

earth or in heaven, making peace by the blood of his cross" (ESV). Thus, when Jesus was born in the manger, he was not only a human infant. He was also truly God, even as he was truly human. He is truly God and truly man forever, the Lord of heaven, the King of kings, descended from his throne. He came to sacrifice everything for the salvation of his people.

Christmas, therefore, is only Christmas if we get our Christology right—our doctrine of Christ. The Bible reveals what the church has defined as the hypostatic union, which describes the unity of two natures in the one person of Jesus Christ. He is true God *and* true man. Jesus did not live as some mere superhuman. His divine nature never diminished at any point during his earthly ministry. He did not inherit a God nature later in his life, nor did his divinity overtake his human nature. From his conception, as the Bible reveals, Jesus was both God and man. This is the fullness we celebrate at Christmas: light has come out of the darkness. God in Christ broke into a fallen world to bring joy, peace, and eternal life.

The audacity of Paul's claim in Colossians 1 would have astounded his original audience. The Roman emperor, Caesar, claimed that he himself was the fullness of deity. Paul's audience, therefore, knew the radical nature of his proclamation that the one true God has only fully dwelt in Jesus Christ of Nazareth. God's fullness was not found in Rome. He did not dwell in a pagan ruler, in a pagan palace, in a pagan city, or in any pagan idol. He dwells fully in his incarnate Son. The fullness of God's presence, the fullness of his nature, the fullness of his power, deity, and reign dwells in Christ and in Christ alone. To whom should the world bend a knee? To whom did the angels shout in glorious praise? It was not Caesar. It was a baby in Bethlehem.

Caesar may have ruled the Roman Empire, but Christ created the cosmos. No particle in the universe exists outside his will. He reigns as Lord over all things, and through him all things were created. From the protons and neutrons to the trillions of stars suspended in the vastness of space, *nothing* exists outside of Christ's authority. The one who slept in the arms of Mary was the same one upholding the heavens and the earth. This is the magnificent, mysterious, yet glorious fullness that Christians proclaim at Christmas. Teach it to your children. Sing of it in your churches. Go and tell the lost of this wonderous truth, for it is the only hope for sinners—and it is a certain hope. A glorious hope.

The Kingdom of
Heaven Is at Hand

*And you, child, will be called the
prophet of the Most High, for you will go
before the Lord to prepare his ways, to
give his people knowledge of salvation
through the forgiveness of their sins.*

Luke 1:76–77

Advent celebrations are often marked by the
exchange of sweet Christmas cards between family
and friends. These often include a picture of the family
and a description of the previous year's activities, along
with an encouragement to join them in worshipping the
Lord Jesus, whose coming we celebrate. Our family has
sent out many such cards over the years to friends and
acquaintances who we have the joy of knowing. Another
familiar practice is for the card to depict some scene

surrounding the birth of Christ. These often beautiful and sentimental Christmas cards may show shepherds, wise men, and a manger scene. We have come to expect these brief greetings commemorating the joyous season.

But have you ever seen a Christmas card that depicts John the Baptist? I certainly doubt it. This would indeed be startling. A man clothed in a garment of camel hair and snacking on locusts and wild honey is not the first image that comes to mind when we imagine the Christmas season.

It is not his appearance but his message that is the primary reason John may feel like an unlikely Christmas character to many. As the one who prepared the way for the coming of Christ in his ministry, John the Baptist proclaimed the essential need for repentance in every human heart. He called on all to recognize and turn from their sin that they might enter the kingdom of God. Can you imagine someone designing a Christmas card featuring John the Baptist? No doubt the accompanying message would need to begin with "Dear Brood of Vipers."

Yet John's message of repentance is, of course, a central component of any meaningful celebration of Christmas. Though it can often be pushed to the background, we need to bring it back to the foreground. In response to God's calling on his life and in anticipation of the appearing of Christ, John the Baptist began to preach in the wilderness of Judea, and he preached what we would rightly understand to be a Christmas sermon. The main point of his preaching was simple yet profound: "Repent, because the kingdom of heaven has come near!" (Matt. 3:2).

This is quite the claim. John urged his hearers to respond to the truth that the presence and promises of God toward his people were being fulfilled among them. Notice also that Jesus issued the same message when he began his own public ministry later in Matthew's Gospel. It is recorded, "From then on Jesus began to preach, 'Repent, because the kingdom of heavens has come near'" (Matt. 4:17). But how could John himself preach this thundering announcement? And why is it appropriate to call it a Christmas sermon?

No doubt, John's father, Zechariah, had been given insight by the Holy Spirit to see the role his son would play in redemption history. He prophesied of him after his birth, saying:

> And you, child, will be called a prophet
> of the Most High, for you will go before
> the Lord to prepare his ways, to give his
> people knowledge of salvation through
> the forgiveness of their sins. Because
> of our God's merciful compassion, the
> dawn from on high will visit us to shine

39

on those who live in darkness and in the
shadow of death, to guide our feet into
the way of peace. (Luke 1:76–79)

John's ministry was to be characterized by his preaching of repentance in preparation for the arrival of the great
guiding light, the presence of God himself. John, furthermore, provided an important foundation for his summons
to repentance: the kingdom of heaven was at hand.

A foundational assumption of the Old Testament is that
God is sovereign over all things, yet the present world is
marred by sin. The conflict between God's right rule and
mankind's rebellion against him fills the pages of the Old
Testament from Genesis to Malachi. God must have his
glory, his people, and his complete dominion over all that
oppose him. This expectation redounds throughout the
Scriptures, and the Old Testament includes the longing of
God's people for the ultimate triumph of Yahweh over all
creation.

The notion of the "kingdom of heaven" represents an
understanding that God's purposes cannot be thwarted and
that he will keep his promises to his people. Not only will
he reign over them, but he will exercise supreme authority
over all mankind. None will ultimately be able to oppose
him. Aspects of this rule had been hinted at and tasted
in the past, but the fullness of it had not yet come. John

proclaims that a great shift has taken place in redemptive history. His message of the kingdom and of repentance is a central message for Christmas.

John's pronouncement about the kingdom was specifically tied to the fact that the Messiah had come. Jesus was soon to step on the scene and begin his public ministry. The kingdom had come because the King had come. This was a declaration of authority and rulership. The long-awaited intervention and reign of God over his people was being fulfilled before their eyes. In these grand movements of redemptive history, God was bringing about—in Christ—the kingdom. And literally, in the following passage, when Jesus himself walks to the Jordan to be baptized by John (Matt. 3:13).

The fiery prophet in camel-hair garments could not have fulfilled his ministry by the Jordan River apart from the incarnation of the Son of God. His preaching of the kingdom's immanence demands a consideration of the manger in Bethlehem. The hopes and dreams of all of God's people find their fulfillment in the coming of Jesus. But the accomplishment of his work doesn't stop in the manger. It includes every moment of his life, building up to his sacrificial death on the cross and glorious resurrection from the dead.

Jesus's victory fulfills and ensures the coming of the fullness of God's reign. Paul tells of the result of Jesus's obedience in death:

> For this reason God highly exalted him and gave him the name that is above every name, so that at the name of Jesus every knew will bow—in heaven and on earth and under the earth—and every tongue will confess that Jesus Christ is Lord, to the glory of God the Father. (Phil. 2:9–11)

Jesus is the embodiment of the kingdom. He is the ruler of the kingdom. He is the presence of the kingdom. The kingdom is his.

What is the fitting response to the glorious first coming of Jesus? The sending of Christmas cards, the exchanging of gifts, the lighting of trees—these are all beautiful and wonderful traditions. But John shows us that, first of all, the right response at Christmas must be repentance.

Entrance into the kingdom Jesus has brought into the world by his coming can only come through a surrender of one's own rebellion to that unshakable kingdom and faith in its eternal King.

A Winnowing Fork
Is in His Hand

"His winnowing fork is in his hand, and
he will clear his threshing floor and gather
his wheat into the barn, but the chaff
he will burn with unquenchable fire."

Matthew 3:12 ESV

Yesterday, we considered an aspect of John the Baptist's Christmas message—that the incarnation of Jesus Christ marks the breaking in of God's righteous and eternal kingdom. John the Baptist added to this declaration another crucial theological truth that deepens our understanding of Jesus's incarnation. In Matthew 3:11–12 (ESV), John the Baptist distinguishes the baptism he brings with what the Messiah will bring. "I baptize you with water for repentance," he proclaimed, "but he who is coming after me is mightier than I, whose sandals I am not worthy to carry. He will baptize you with the Holy Spirit and

43

fire. His winnowing fork is in his hand, and he will clear his threshing floor and gather his wheat into the barn, but the chaff he will burn with unquenchable fire." How's that for a Christmas sermon?

Thus, the coming of Christ, as John preaches, is certainly a cause for great joy but only for those who submit to him and revel in his grace. In other words, the coming of the Messiah is also an announcement of the judgment that is to come.

Indeed, later in Matthew's Gospel, Jesus speaks of his own ministry as being a sword that divides, even down to the ties of family. That which will set "a man against his father, and a daughter against her mother" (Matt. 10:35) and will be the measure of his disciples' love for him (Matt. 10:37). This dividing will take place ultimately in the final judgment when, as Jesus described, "he will separate people one from another as a shepherd separates the sheep from the goats" (Matt. 25:32 ESV).

Picturing Christ as holding a winnowing fork is the powerful agricultural image we are given in John's sermon. Before the advent of combines and mechanical harvesters, this tool was used to throw wheat into the air in order that the wind might drive away the light chaff, the unwanted hulls. If you have ever driven across the great plains of the United States during harvest season, then you have a modern-day demonstration of this sifting taking place. As the wheat or other grains are collected within the combine, the chaff is spit out the back of the machine, much of it being blown around by the wind. The winnowing fork is a symbol of judgment.

Mark this: Jesus Christ will judge all mankind. His first coming has announced the reality of this future judgment. He has not first appeared with his winnowing fork visibly in hand but rather as a suffering servant who lived just like we do yet without sin. He told of this time of future judgment, but its fullness did not arrive during his earthly ministry. John declares it here in Matthew 3, and Jesus speaks of it often in the Gospels, but we are still awaiting its fullness. The reminder of that judgment which is to come is ever present, such that John the Baptist is able to declare in the present, "His winnowing fork is in his hand" (Matt. 3:12 ESV). He holds the means of his judging at the ready, and so all must prepare for that day of judgment.

Reflecting on the manger and the cross is rightly common at Christmas among Christians, but what about the notion of our Savior holding an agricultural harvest tool as an image of divine judgment? This image demands that we consider the proper response to the truths of the incarnation. Jesus has come. He was born. Not only that, but he lived, he died, he was raised from the dead, he ascended to the right hand of the Father, and he will return as judge.

John the Baptist makes clear that our first response to those Christmas truths must be repentance of sins—a turning from the kingdom of self to the kingdom of God. A course correction in response to the arrival of the One who came for us and for our salvation, whom John foretold. We cannot enter into his kingdom apart from this reconciliation with a holy God.

My plea is that Christ's church would preach and proclaim a Christmas message of repentance. A true Christmas means that in this season we all must testify to the necessity of responding appropriately to the coming of Christ. We can only truly join in the chorus of "Joy to the World" if we have been cleansed of our sin and are no longer under the threat of the fiery judgment that is to come. Christmas reminds us all that Jesus was born in Bethlehem as a baby. But when Christ returns, he will come as a conquering King and will execute judgment—perfect judgment. As we proclaim repentance, we ourselves serve as a sort of winnowing fork in the Savior's hand, testifying to what is to come.

You might object that Christmas is not a time for speaking of judgment and repentance but only of the love and rejoicing the season represents. But we cannot put different aspects of the gospel into conflict. We must preach the whole gospel all the time, or we risk speaking a different gospel, which, as Paul reminds us, is really no gospel at all (Gal. 1:7). Heralding the good news of Jesus Christ necessarily entails calling people to repent of their sins. Repentance, which is only made possible through the sacrificial death of Jesus Christ and the empowerment of the Holy Spirit (Rom. 8:12–13), presses the unbeliever to turn away from that which brings death in order to embrace that which brings life, joy, and peace. A failure to call the unbeliever to repent is, in short, a failure to share the gospel. It is motivated out of fear rather than love. It also veils one of the most precious gifts the gospel brings to those who believe, namely, the freedom to live as a child of the living God (Gal. 5:1).

Perhaps now you'll more readily think of John the Baptist as a Christmas character. Maybe you'll even include him on the front of your Christmas card for next year. Reminded of John's message, may we commit ourselves to heralding Christ's postmanger message in light of the cross: "Repent, because the kingdom of heaven has come near!" (Matt. 3:2). Only then can we know a truly merry Christmas, indeed.

Yearning for Deliverance

Then a shoot will grow from the stump of
Jesse, and a branch from his roots will bear
fruit. The Spirit of the LORD will rest on him.

Isaiah 11:1—2

U nderstood rightly, the entire Bible is the Christmas story. Rightly understood, there is no text in all the Scriptures that does not relate to Christmas as a glorious event of promise, fulfillment, and future hope. In fact, the Gospels of Matthew, Luke, and John all frame their accounts of the birth of Jesus with a look back to the Old Testament—connecting the advent of Christ with the totality of God's sovereign purpose to bring salvation to his people. If we want to deepen our understanding of Christmas, we need to see how the coming of the Messiah happened only after thousands of years of hopeful expectation. If we want to recapture the glory of Christmas, we must see how God, despite human sin and depravity, providentially orchestrated all the events of history to bring about the birth of his Son. We need to become a people who *yearn*—a people who *long* for God to make all things new. Christmas affords us an opportunity to do just that as we consider the longing experience of God's people as they looked for the coming messiah.

The prophet Isaiah poetically described a branch that would be "a shoot will grow from the stump of Jesse" (Isa. 11:1). This promised branch will not only bear much fruit, but it will never die. As the rest of the chapter continues, Isaiah discloses that this shoot will rid the entire cosmos from the realities of the curse. The devastation of sin will be no more as the creation itself will be set right: "They will not hurt or destroy each other," as Isaiah proclaimed, "on my entire holy mountain, for the land will be as full of the knowledge of the LORD as the sea is filled with water" (Isa. 11:9).

We read these prophetic declarations with hindsight on our side. We live on the side of fulfillment. While we should live in constant gratitude that we are in the age of the church, our sense of the promises fulfilled can rob us of something Isaiah and his original audience would have experienced as they considered these promises of God for the first time: *yearning*. The promise of the shoot from the stump of Jesse would have sprouted hope and longing in Isaiah. A yearning for peace, justice, and the perennial kingdom would have filled the hearts of all those who heeded his messages. How else could they have responded when they considered that this branch, this promised Messiah, would delight in the fear of the Lord and bring redemption to the people of God? How else would they respond as they pondered a day when the Lord would be the delight of his people and the fear of the Lord would be made known to all? How else should they respond as Isaiah described the reversal of the curse and the end of sin?

Christmas undoubtedly is a time of enormous and unfathomable joy at the coming of the promised Son. And yet we should also let this season fill us with yearning—a yearning similar to what Isaiah and his audience would have felt when they looked upon the state of Israel and longed for the day when Yahweh would intervene. Indeed, we stand on the other side of the baby in the manger. We celebrate this Christmas the fulfillment of what Isaiah only envisioned. We can look back on the birth of Christ as the moment when the shoot from the stump of Jesse appeared. Despite this, we are still a people who *need* to yearn. We still look forward to the fullness of these promises found in Isaiah. We ought to long for the coming of the King of kings and Lord of lords. Christmas reminds us of the yearning of Israel for the coming Messiah. Christmas also reminds us that we are awaiting his second coming.

Our yearning should only intensify during the Christmas season. We should, as Isaiah revealed in Isaiah 11, yearn for the fullness of the messianic reign, when the wolf will dwell with the lamb and the leopard with the goat. On that day the carnivores will kill no more. The world will no longer be divided between predators and prey, living by the law of eat or be eaten. The bear will graze with the cow. The lion will eat hay with the ox. All things will be as they were intended before the fall of mankind into darkness. When the light of Christ comes, the nursing child shall play over the hole of the cobra, and the weaned child shall put his hand on the adder's den. Do not try that at home, of course—not until the Lord comes to establish his kingdom in fullness. In this age, keep your babies away from the cobras and adders. We are not yet in that peaceable, eternal kingdom, but one day we will be. One day the entire creation and all God's people will dwell in common rest, common peace, and common trust.

That is a day for which we should surely yearn. Without yearning, we forget the faithfulness of God and lose sight of our ultimate destination. This Christmas, let your hearts be full of joy with the coming of the Son, but don't neglect yearning and longing. Christ has come. He will come again, and we should await that day with conscious eagerness, expectation, and hope.

Why the Incarnation?

For in bringing many sons and daughters
to glory, it was entirely appropriate that
God—for whom and through whom all
things exist—should make the pioneer of
their salvation perfect through sufferings.
For the one who sanctifies and those
who are sanctified all have one Father.
That is why Jesus is not ashamed to call
them brothers and sisters, saying:
I will proclaim your name to
my brothers and sisters;
I will sing hymns to you in the congregation.
Again, I will trust in him. And again, Here
I am with the children God gave me.
Now since the children have flesh and
blood in common, Jesus also shared in

53

these, so that through his death he might
destroy the one holding the power of
death—that is, the devil—and free those
who were held in slavery all their lives
by the fear of death. For it is clear that
he does not reach out to help angels, but
to help Abraham's offspring. Therefore,
he had to be like his brothers and sisters
in every way, so that he could become a
merciful and faithful high priest in matters
pertaining to God, to make atonement for
the sins of the people. For since he himself
has suffered when he was tempted, he
is able to help those who are tempted.

Hebrews 2:10—18

The book of Hebrews boldly declares the glory of the new covenant over the covenant of old. Indeed, Hebrews instructs us to behold the radiant Christ and his superiority over the Mosaic law. As such, the book of Hebrews draws our attention to the ministry and mission of Jesus Christ. As the Son of God, Christ is superior to the angels. Unlike the priests of the old covenant, Jesus's sinless perfection enabled him to stand as a perfect mediator between God and the people—indeed, he reigns forever as the Great High Priest. Unlike the animal sacrifices of Israel's history, Jesus laid his own life down as the perfect, spotless lamb. Every moment of Jesus's life, every aspect of his ministry, surpassed the old covenant and established a new and eternal covenant of redemption.

Hebrews begins with an immediate declaration of Christ's superiority. The author of the book wrote, "Long ago, at many times and in many ways, God spoke to our fathers by the prophets, but in these last days he has spoken to us by his Son, whom he appointed the heir of all things, through whom also he created the world" (Heb. 1:1–2 ESV). God veiled himself in the old covenant. He spoke through intermediaries—through the law, the prophets, and the angels. Now, however, God incarnate has come. God now speaks through his own eternal Son. God is not silent. He reveals himself because he loves those to whom he reveals himself.

Verse 2 reveals that the Son has also been appointed heir of all things. In other words, when the Son appeared, he appeared with the glory of the Father. The words "heir of all things" denote royal language. In a few short words, the author reveals that when Jesus came, he was no intermediary, he was no angel, he was no mere prophet. The baby in the manger—Son of God and Son of Man—reigned

as Creator of the cosmos and the heir of the heavenly kingdom. He entered the world he had made. He had fashioned
the arms that held him. He made the wood that framed his
manger. He made the entire cosmos, and yet he came as a
tiny infant. Christmas celebrates the startling yet spectacular truth embedded in the incarnation. Specifically,
Hebrews 2 points to the meaning of the incarnation and the
need of all humanity for God to send his only Son.

Read again the passage above and consider how it
gets to the heart of the incarnation and distills the glory
of Christmas. Jesus Christ, the eternal Son of God, took
on flesh to identify with us—a broken, sinful, rebellious,
lost people who sold ourselves to the power of Satan.
Furthermore, Jesus identified with us in *every* respect.
These verses declare the lavishness of Christ's love for his
people. Jesus must be made like us in every way yet without
sin. Without the incarnation, therefore, humanity stands
condemned. Without the blood of the perfect Son of God,
humanity remains under the wrath of God's judgment.
Without the incarnate Son, mankind has no mediator—no
perfect priest to make atonement on our behalf. Without
the God-man, there is no hope. Why the incarnation?
Because without it, *all* humanity perishes forever.

Indeed, Hebrews 2 unveils the impeccable beauty of
the Word of God who took on flesh. It summons us to a
vision of Christmas that far surpasses *anything* our culture

could piece together about the meaning and purpose of this season. Jesus, the Son of God, "had to be like his brothers and sisters," according to Hebrews 2:17. How could the Creator of the world, the second person of the trinity, refer to redeemed sinners as his brothers? The incarnation, in a spectacular display of divine grace, constituted a familial act of God: he did not come to make us his servants and slaves; he came to bring us into his family—to adoption as sons and daughters of God.

The familial goal of Christmas had long been foretold. Indeed, the author of Hebrews, in 2:12, quotes Psalm 22:22: "I will proclaim your name to my brothers and sisters; I will sing hymns to you in the congregation." Hebrews juxtaposes Psalm 22 with the necessity of the incarnation. In so doing, the author brings the entire context of Psalm 22 into his argument—Psalm 22 being the famous Messianic Psalm which begins, "My God, my God, why have you abandoned me?" (v. 1). The imagery evoked by the author of Hebrews could not be more potent. The incarnation's goal aimed at the cross. The birth of Christ only began the mission. From the moment of Jesus's birth, he progressed, minute by minute, to the culminating act of his entire ministry: his suffering on the cross. Through his suffering and death, he founded salvation for the people of God. Through the shedding of his pure blood, he served as the one source of perfect sanctification. By drawing upon the rich wells of Psalm 22, the author of Hebrews powerfully displays the goal of the incarnation—indeed the goal of Christmas. Christ came to die. In dying, however, he established a new family—not an ethnic family descending from the nation of Israel but a family knit together by faith in Jesus Christ. When Jesus came, he made us, as the author of Hebrews notes, his brothers. He came to tell his family about the glory of the Father and the way to be reconciled to him.

This passage rings loudly the glory of Christmas and the wonder of the incarnation. By becoming like us, Christ made himself our brother, securing our adoption into the household of God. By becoming like us, he promises to make all things new—indeed, his birth, life, death, resurrection, and ascension secured a glorious inheritance for God's people. This inheritance will never fade or perish. It will be nothing less than all things made new, even our bodies.

Finally, by becoming like us, Jesus established his priesthood. God incarnate served as a priest that eclipsed the priesthood of the Old Testament. He entered the heavenly temple into the presence of God and laid his own life down on the mercy seat. He shed his own blood for God's people. Now he sits at God's right hand and intercedes on our behalf. By becoming like us, he knows our weaknesses and fears; he is well acquainted with the trials we face. Thus, he lives as a high priest who beckons all to run to him and find rest. As Jesus said in Matthew 11:28, "Come to me, all of you who are weary and burdened, and I will give you rest." By virtue of his incarnation, he became the high priest that not only secured our salvation but fills us with his power and grace. This is, indeed, the spectacular glory of Christmas. Come and adore this glorious priest, this incarnate Son, who took on flesh for you and for me.

Must We Believe in the Virgin Birth?

Therefore, the Lord himself will give you a sign. Behold, the virgin shall conceive and bear a son, and shall call his name Immanuel.

Isaiah 7:14 ESV

"She will bear a son, and you shall call his name Jesus, for he will save his people from their sins." All this took place to fulfill what the Lord had spoken by the prophet: "Behold, the virgin shall conceive and bear a son, and they shall call his name Immanuel" (which means, God with us).

Matthew 1:21–23 ESV

Must one believe in the virgin birth to be a Christian? This is not a hard question to answer. It is conceivable that someone might come to Christ and trust Christ as Savior without yet learning that the Bible teaches Jesus was born of a virgin. A new believer is not yet aware of the full structure of Christian truth. The real question is this: Can a Christian, once aware of the Bible's teaching, *reject* the virgin birth? The answer must be no.

In one of his columns for the *New York Times*, Nicholas Kristof once pointed to belief in the virgin birth as evidence that conservative Christians are "less intellectual." Are we saddled with an untenable doctrine? Kristof, for example, pointed to his grandfather as a "devout" Presbyterian elder who believed that the virgin birth is a "pious legend." Follow his example, Kristof encourages, and join the modern age.[5] But we must face the hard fact that a denial of the virgin birth is a denial of the Christian faith.

The aversion toward the virgin birth has long infiltrated American public discourse. On April 11, 1823, Thomas Jefferson wrote a letter to John Adams in which he discussed his views concerning Jesus Christ. Jefferson was already known for his denial of miracles and other claims of supernatural intervention in history and nature. In this letter to John Adams, he predicted the collapse of all belief in the virgin birth of Christ: "And the day will come when the mystical generation of Jesus, by the supreme being as his father in the womb of a virgin will be classed with the fable of the generation of Minerva in the brain of Jupiter. But we may hope that the dawn of reason and freedom of thought in these United States will do away with all this artificial scaffolding, and restore to us the primitive and genuine doctrines of this the most venerated reformer of human errors."[6]

Theological liberals deny the virgin birth as revealed truth; Thomas Jefferson saw the Gospel accounts as "artificial scaffolding," and many modern Americans increasingly see the virgin birth as part of a "theological story" about Jesus.

Back in the early decades of the twentieth century, when theological liberals such as Harry Emerson Fosdick were denying the virgin birth, Baptist New Testament scholar A. T. Robertson rose to its defense. In a little 1925 book, *The Mother of Jesus*, Robertson isolated the alternatives: affirm the truth of the virgin conception of Christ or abandon any claim of incarnation.[7]

Robertson, who was among the most famous scholars of his day, taught at The Southern Baptist Theological Seminary from 1888 until 1934. He understood exactly what was at stake. The modernists, as theological liberals liked to be known, accepted a distinction between the "Jesus of history" and the "Christ of faith." They wanted to present a Jesus worthy of moral emulation but not a supernatural Christ who was God in human flesh. In between, theological "moderates" attempted a compromise between orthodoxy and heresy, offering a Jesus who was supernatural but not *too* supernatural. They were eager to reject the virgin birth but tried to hold to other facts of the incarnation. Robertson saw through both the modernists and the moderates. Neither presented a Jesus who was truly God in human flesh.

As Robertson understood, the virgin conception of Christ is both fundamental and necessary to the New Testament's presentation of Christ.

He also saw what others try not to admit: if Jesus was not conceived by the Holy Spirit, then he had a human father. Without the virgin birth, there is no explanation for the incarnation. If Jesus had a merely human father, there is no authentic connection to the incarnational theology of Paul and John in the New Testament. All that remains is some attempt to claim that Jesus was a mere human being who had a unique divine mission, or who was uniquely God conscious, or who was somehow adopted by the Father into a form of deity. All of these are heretical christs, and none of these can save. Christmas, then, is no season of joy and glad tidings because we are still lost in sin.

Matthew tells us that "it was discovered before [Mary and Joseph] came together that she was pregnant from the Holy Spirit" (Matt. 1:18). This, Matthew explains, fulfilled what Isaiah promised: "'See, the virgin will become pregnant and give birth to a son, and they will name him Immanuel,' which is translated 'God with us'" (Matt. 1:23; cf. Isa. 7:14).

Luke provides even greater detail, revealing that Mary was visited by an angel who explained that she, though a virgin, would bear the divine child: "The Holy Spirit will come upon you, and the power of the Most High will overshadow you. Therefore, the holy one to be born will be called the Son of God" (Luke 1:35).

Even if the virgin birth was taught by only one biblical passage, that would be sufficient to obligate all Christians to the belief. We have no right to weigh the relative truthfulness of biblical teachings by their repetition in Scripture. We cannot claim to believe the Bible is the Word of God and then turn around and cast suspicion on its teaching.

Many of our neighbors may find belief in the virgin birth to be evidence of intellectual backwardness among American Christians. But this is the faith of the church, established in God's perfect Word, and cherished by the true church throughout the ages. Those who deny the virgin birth affirm other doctrines only by force of whim, for they have already surrendered the authority of Scripture. They have undermined Christ's nature and nullified the incarnation.

Many of our unbelieving neighbors want to have "Jingle Bells" and all the rest, but when it comes to singing about the God of the universe in human flesh—in Bethlehem's manger—suddenly some get a little lump in their throat and can't go any further. They all of a sudden find those are the words they do not want to sing.

This much we know: all those who find salvation will be saved by the atoning work of Jesus the Christ, the virgin-born Savior. Anything less than this is just not Christianity, whatever it may call itself. A true Christian will not deny the virgin birth. We are saved because Jesus Christ was, just as Scripture reveals, born of a virgin, born to Mary. We have to sing this truth as glorious as all others.

And Them that Mourn

The people walking in darkness have
seen a great light; a light has dawned on
those living in the land of darkness.

Isaiah 9:2

Families across the Christian world gather for Christmas even now, with caravans of cars and planeloads of passengers headed to hearth and home. Christmas comes once again, filled with the joy, expectation, and sentiment of the season.

And yet the sentiment and joy of the season are often accompanied by different emotions and memories. At some point, every Christian home is invaded by the pressing memory of loved ones who can no longer gather—of empty chairs and empty arms and aching hearts. For some, the grief is fresh, suffering the death of one who was present at the Christmas gathering last year but is now among the saints resting in Christ. For others, it is the grief of a loss suffered long ago. We grieve the absence of parents and grandparents and aunts and uncles and siblings. Some, with a grief almost too great to bear, suffer the heartbreak that comes with the death of a child.

For all of us, the knowledge of recent events, of unspeakable horror, and the murder of young children makes us think of so many homes with such overwhelming grief.

Is Christmas also for those who grieve? Such a question would perplex those who experienced the events that night in humble Bethlehem and those who followed Christ throughout his earthly ministry. *Christmas is especially for those who grieve.*

The apostle Paul, writing to the Galatians, reminds us of the fact that we are born as slaves to sin. "When the time came to completion, God sent his Son, born of a woman, born under the law, to redeem those under the law, so that we might receive adoption as sons" (Gal. 4:4–5). Out of darkness came light. As the prophet Isaiah foretold, "The people walking in darkness have seen a great light; a light has dawned on those living in the land of darkness" (Isa. 9:2).

This same Christ is the Messiah who, as Isaiah declared, "has borne our griefs and carried our sorrows" (Isa. 53:4 ESV). He fully identifies with and shares all our afflictions, and he came that we might know the only rescue from death, sorrow, grief, and sin.

The baby Jesus was born into a world of grief, suffering, and loss. The meaning of his incarnation was recognized by the aged Zechariah, the father of John the Baptist, who prophesied that God had acted to save his people: "Because of our God's merciful compassion, the dawn from on high will visit us to shine on those who live in darkness and the shadow of death, to guide our feet into the way of peace" (Luke 1:78–79).

There are so many Christians who, even now, are suffering the grief that feels much like the shadow of death. How can they celebrate Christmas, and how might we celebrate with them?

In 1918, a special service was written for the choir of King's College at Great Britain's Cambridge University. The "Festival of Nine Lessons and Carols" was first read and sung in the magnificent chapel of King's College in that same year, establishing what is now a venerable Christmas tradition. In the "Bidding Prayer" prepared to call the congregation together for that beautiful service, the great truths of Christmas are declared in unforgettable prose:

> Beloved in Christ, be it this Christmas
> Eve our care and delight to prepare our-
> selves to hear again the message of the

Angels, and in heart and mind to go even unto Bethlehem and see this thing which is come to pass, and the Babe lying in a manger.

Therefore let us hear again from Holy Scripture the tale of the loving purposes of God from the first days of our sin unto the glorious Redemption brought us by this Holy Child. . . .

But first, . . . let us pray . . . for the needs of the whole world . . . ; for peace upon the earth . . . ; for love and unity within the one Church He did build, and especially in this city; for brotherhood and goodwill amongst all men. . . .

Let us remember before Him the poor, the cold, the hungry, the oppressed; the sick and them that mourn; the lonely and the unloved; the aged and the little children; all those who know not the Lord Jesus, or who love Him not, or who by sin have grieved His heart of love.[8]

On the evening of the celebration of Christ's birth, Christians are called to remember, in Christ's name, the poor and the helpless, the cold and the hungry, the oppressed and the sick, the lonely and the unloved, the aged and the children, those who do not know Christ, "and them that mourn."

The church is filled with those who, while not grieving as others grieve, bear grief as Christians who miss their loved ones, who cherish their memories, and who wonder at times how to think of such grief at Christmas. Far too many homes are filled with *them that mourn*.

And it will be so until Christ comes again. The great truth of Christmas is that the Father so loved the world that he sent his own Son to assume human flesh and to dwell among us, to die for our sins and to suffer for our iniquity, and to declare that the kingdom of God is at hand. This same Jesus was raised from the dead on the third day, conquering death and sin. There is salvation, full pardon from sin, and life everlasting to those who believe and trust in him.

Christmas is especially for those who mourn and suffer grief, for the message of Christmas is nothing less than the death of death in the death and resurrection of Christ.

Christmas is especially for those bearing grief and sorrow. Our joy is hindered temporarily by the loss we have suffered, even as we know that those who are in Christ are promised everlasting life. We know that even now they are with Christ, for "to be absent from the body [is] to be present with the Lord" (2 Cor. 5:8 KJV). It was Christ himself who promised that our "sorrow will turn to joy" (John 16:20).

That Bidding Prayer written for King's College draws to a close with words that speak so powerfully to the church about these truths: "Lastly let us remember before Him them who rejoice with us, but upon another shore, and in a greater light, that multitude which no man can number, whose hope was in the Word made flesh, and with whom, in this Lord Jesus, we forever more are one."9

Those words are exactly right. Those who have gone before us to be with the Lord are with us in Christmas joy. They rejoice with us "but upon another shore, and in a greater light." Our loved ones in Christ are in that unnumbered multitude "whose hope was in the Word made flesh." The great truth of Christmas is shouted in the face of death when we declare that, even now, "in this Lord Jesus we forever more are one."10

Your loved one was not created and given the gift of life merely for that chair now empty. Those who are in Christ were created for eternal glory. We must train our sentiments to lean into truth, and we must know that Christmas is especially for those who grieve.

The chair may be now empty, but heaven will be full. Remember, above all else, that those who are in Christ, though dead, celebrate Christmas with us—just upon another shore, and in a greater light.

14

Our Peace in the Promises of God

*Bethlehem Ephrathah, you are small among
the clans of Judah; one will come from you
to be ruler over Israel for me. His origin
is from antiquity, from ancient times.*

Micah 5:2

He will be their peace.

Micah 5:5

Interestingly, some of our most cherished Christmas carols are not actually Christmas carols, which is to say that some of the great hymns associated with Christmas were written for the church to sing all year round. Christians often long for the season when the church sings these hymns (and *when* it is appropriate to start singing Christmas carols is no small debate among Christians). An example of such a hymn is "Joy to the World." This hymn is written about the coming of the Lord to judge the earth and is based on Psalm 98. Yet these grand truths have been applied to the Lord's coming to Bethlehem, so the hymn has become a Christmas hymn and cherished as a carol.

Christians do not just sing such songs because of the melody or the nostalgia they invoke. Although such a hymn's tune may resonate or remind us of great memories, hymns like "Joy to the World" are meaningful because of their great truths—because of the theological weight and power they declare. We sing these songs because they remind us of the truth, which enables faithful living in our homes, churches, and communities. This is what Christmas time is about anyway, as Christians gather to rejoice over the revelation of the gospel. Because of the truth revealed in Bethlehem so many years ago, Christians eagerly and joyfully celebrate, trust, and embrace the truths of Scripture and our Lord, Jesus Christ.

Christmas hymns like "Joy to the World" contain lyrics about the promises of God. As such, these hymns, by the power of God's Spirit, evoke within us longing, hope, and faith in our God who alone can keep his promises and keep them perfectly. The glory of Christmas, therefore, is heightened as we consider the joy God's people are to have as they remember his promises and the peace such remembrance brings.

In the Old Testament, despite great tribulations, faithful Israelites searched for the coming Savior because they trusted God's Word and promises. After the great times of David and Solomon, king after king collapsed under the weight of his sin and brought the nation down with him. Eventually, the humiliation of Jerusalem arrived as it gave way to siege, and the nations of Israel and Judah were carried away into captivity. Such terrible circumstances made the Israelites' search for their Savior desperate in a new way. Before the worst had even come and Israel and Judah collapsed into exile, God sent the prophet Micah to assure his people that his word could be trusted. Micah decried the moral state of the nation of Israel, but he also prophesied great hope in the coming of the Lord as his people's Savior. He declared, "Now you muster your troops, O daughter of troops; siege is laid against us; with a rod they strike the judge of Israel on the cheek. But you, O Bethlehem Ephrathah, who are too little to be among the clans of Judah, from you shall come forth for me one who is to be ruler in Israel, whose coming forth is from of old, from ancient days. . . . And he shall be their peace" (Mic. 5:1–2, 5 ESV).

Peace is what the Israelites long hoped for, and the nation's rejection of God and his commands made abundantly clear that they had looked in the wrong places for peace. The story of the people of Israel demonstrates humanity's need to embrace God alone for the peace they desired. In fact, the context of Micah 5 is the persecution and alienation of God's people. They hungered for the one who would come and rescue them from humiliation and restore Israel to its glory. In this passage, the Lord, through the prophet Micah, assures his people that rescue is coming, and it will come from Bethlehem.

We know Bethlehem. We have hymns at this time of year about this little town in Israel. Bethlehem is also the city of David. God sent Samuel to anoint Israel's next king to rescue Israel from the tragedy of King Saul, and God sent Samuel specifically to Jesse's house. God did not want Samuel to anoint any of the older sons of Jesse but a little boy still out in the fields shepherding the sheep. That little boy is King David, and Jesse's house is in Bethlehem. God had already rescued his people from the seemingly insignificant Bethlehem through an unassuming savior. God would do it again, and the prophet Micah, used by God, became the vehicle for telling the children of God that rescue would come. Christians also know that even though God was going to send rescue from Bethlehem through an initially unassuming man, he would not rescue them in the same way. This next rescue would not merely be like what was represented in King David. We know this is King Jesus. The people were right to embrace the rescue of King David, and they would have been right to embrace the promise of the coming Savior. King Jesus would bring the peace the people so desperately desired.

Micah's message encouraged the people of God, reminding them of his grace and mercy. He told them they could trust in God's sovereign purposes and his insurmountable power to enact his promises. This not only instilled within the people of Israel greater assurance in God, but it also nourished a peculiar peace. Even though they faced persecution, and the nation had been ravaged by the nations, they could remain a people of peace because of the God they worshipped. They could trust that Yahweh would bring peace not just to Israel but also to the ends of the earth.

But the peace promised in this passage was not merely a sociopolitical peace. It was a promise of *peace with God*, which is exactly why we celebrate the incarnation. Christians today celebrate the promises of God and the fulfillment of those promises because they are not merely about a rescue from the humiliation of Jerusalem. Christians know we need to be rescued from our sin. Because of the truth revealed in the Christmas story, we are rescued by Jesus. He was humiliated so that we might become children of God. He humbled himself so that we might draw near to the throne of grace. He became like us so that we might be called his brothers and sisters. He suffered and died for us. He suffered and died to secure our peace with God.

This rescue from sin brings ultimate, unshakable peace, and in this rescue alone peace can be found. This truth is common in the New Testament. When Paul writes in Ephesians 2:14 that Christ Jesus is our peace, he means that Jesus Christ accomplished, in himself, in his shed blood, in his own body, in his substitutionary atonement, the peace we could never achieve. He achieved a peace we could not achieve individually for all who are his own, a peace we could never achieve even temporarily. He achieves eternal peace and fulfills his promise. If the people of Israel wanted peace, this was the truth they needed to embrace, and if anyone today wants peace, they must believe this same truth.

And because of this truth, we can truly sing "Joy to the world!" We love to sing the great Christmas hymns precisely because they are *true*.

15

The Good Shepherd

*And he shall stand and shepherd his
flock in the strength of the LORD, in the
majesty of the name of the LORD his God.
And they shall dwell secure, for now he
shall be great to the ends of the earth.*

Micah 5:4 ESV

*In the same region shepherds were staying
out in the fields and keeping watch at night
over their flock. Then an angel of the Lord
stood before them, and the glory of the Lord
shone around them, and they were terrified.*

Luke 2:8–9

*"I am the good shepherd. The good
shepherd lays down his life for the sheep."*

John 10:11

Yesterday, we considered the prophetic words of Micah 5 and its importance in pointing not only to the coming incarnation of the Son of Man but also to the peace provided in the promises of God. Micah's prophecy, however, included another crucial theme—a theme full of significance as it relates to biblical theology and to the glory of Christmas.

Micah, by God's direction, revealed that the coming Messiah from Bethlehem would also be a shepherd king. It would have been just as right for the people of Old Testament times to celebrate the promise that he would be a shepherd as it would be right for Christians today to celebrate this same reality. Indeed, the image of a shepherd and the promise that the Messiah was to come from Bethlehem pointed Israel back to an important moment in salvation history. When the prophet Samuel went to the house of Jesse, the Bethlehemite, he looked for which of his sons should be anointed king of Israel. Outward appearances enticed Samuel to anoint many of the candidates that initially appeared before him, but God kept telling him no. The king to be—the king after God's own heart—was not the oldest, tallest, or most handsome. It was the youngest son, and he was busy, faithfully tending to his father's flock. The shepherd boy was chosen as Israel's greatest king (1 Sam. 16:1–13).

When David became king, was he no longer a shepherd? Not hardly. Israel was to have a shepherd king who would shepherd the people, protecting them from enemies seeking to devour them. The promises of God come together at Christmas in the Shepherd King. Micah 5:4 states that his Shepherd's role will be demonstrated in the fact that he shall stand. That is so important—*he shall stand*. In other words, this is *the* ruler. He has been raised, and as he stands, he will shepherd his flock in the strength of the Lord.

His shepherding rule, moreover, will never fade or pass away. Nothing will overpower the coming Shepherd who will guide God's people, and he will *always* be our Shepherd. As Micah declared, the coming Shepherd will be a ruler whose origin is from old, from ancient days (Mic. 5:2). In other words, this is not just the reestablishment in a human sense of the dynasty of David. This ruler will come forth from of old—from ancient days, indeed from eternity past. This makes sense to us two thousand years after the birth of the Lord, Jesus Christ in Bethlehem. This makes sense to us as we can connect, understand, and see the fulfillment of God's promises. Israel must have received these words with such hope and celebration. Christians receive those exact words with even better understanding and the same hope and celebration.

Indeed, when Micah 5 is placed within the course of redemptive history and understood in light of the incarnation, this promise of a Good Shepherd becomes all the more important for us as we celebrate Christmas. This promised Shepherd would not just provide physical protection for his people. Jesus would come as the Good Shepherd, the one who would rescue us from our sin and protect us from the devil. He comes to secure us in his pasture forever. As revealed in John 10:11, Jesus is the Shepherd King who has come to lay his life down for his people. He shepherds his flock. He loses not one of his sheep. He lovingly shepherds his people, the flock of God. That does not mean just a little flock of sinners. It means a little flock of Christ's sheep saved by grace. Jesus is our Shepherd King, and we can trust a King who cares for his people as shepherds care for their sheep. The Shepherd loves his sheep. The Good Shepherd gave his life for his sheep.

In this light, it is fascinating to consider who first heard the news of the birth of Christ as a baby in Bethlehem. It was just common shepherds watching their flock in the darkness. As Luke records, "In the same region, shepherds were staying out in the fields and keeping watch at night over their flock. Then an angel of the Lord stood before them, and the glory of the Lord shone around them, and they were terrified" (Luke 2:8–9). These first witnesses to the birth of the Good Shepherd in Bethlehem were themselves shepherds. To them was given the astounding truth, "Unto you is born this day in the city of David a Savior, who is Christ the Lord" (Luke 2:11 ESV). They went to see what the angels had told them, and then they went and told others, unable to keep to themselves the glorious news that the Christ was born (Luke 2:15–20). We would do well to follow their example—to proclaim to everyone we encounter the good news of the Good Shepherd, who has come to save us from our sins.

What we celebrate this Christmas season, what we observe with our eyes, and what we feel so joyously in our hearts is a promise that God is building his church and protecting her by the power of the Good Shepherd. In the church, through the sovereignty of the Lord Jesus Christ and through the earthen vessels he commissions for the preaching of the Word, the flock will be fed in the strength of the Lord. This gives us such cause for rejoicing. It makes us want to pray, and it makes us want to sing. Let us always rejoice in everything we do during this Christmas, and may we be reminded of what a tremendous, infinite gift God has given us in Jesus Christ.

We celebrate Christmas because what Micah promised long ago has been fulfilled. Jesus Christ is standing and feeding his flock. That is Christ's messianic rule. He is the Ruler who was promised. He was born in Bethlehem, but he commissioned his people to declare the glory of his gospel.

Because he, to all people everywhere, reigns, Christians can eagerly and joyfully celebrate, trust, and embrace the truths of Scripture and our Lord, Jesus Christ. And so, our commitment this Christmas season must be to this as we stand in the strength of the Lord.

How Beautiful upon the Mountains Are the Feet of Him Who Brings Good News

How beautiful upon the mountains are
the feet of him who brings good news, who
publishes peace, who brings good news
of happiness, who publishes salvation,
who says to Zion, "Your God reigns."

Isaiah 52:7 ESV

T he celebration of the nativity of Christ comes with triumphant declarations, prophesies, songs of praise, the good news of the gospel, and a spectacular opportunity for maximum theological clarity. I mean the kind of clarity the shepherds heard from the angelic host who declared that a child has been born in the city of David, a Savior, who is Christ the Lord. The clarity of Simeon, who announced when he held the infant Christ, "For my eyes have seen your salvation. You have prepared it in the presence of all peoples" (Luke 2:30–31). The clarity of Mary, who declared, "the Mighty One has done great things for me, and his name is holy" (Luke 1:49).

We live in a day of dangerous theological confusion—a day when that confusion comes from far too many pulpits and lecterns and churches. Christmas stands as the great biblical refutation of that confusion. A simple reading of the Gospel accounts of the birth of Jesus presents declarative sentences, undeniable truth claims that come with unavoidable clarity.

Indeed, Luke 1:67–79 distills how powerfully the gospel is declared in Jesus's birth. In it Luke recounts Zechariah's prophecy upon the birth of his son, John. God had struck Zechariah mute because he did not believe God would grant Zechariah and his wife a son. At John's birth, however, God opened Zechariah's mouth, and the Spirit prophesied through him. As Zechariah stated, "And you, child, will be called the prophet of the Most High, for you will go before the Lord to prepare his ways, to give his people knowledge of salvation through the forgiveness of their sins. Because of our God's merciful compassion" (Luke 1:76–78).

Zechariah knew John would prepare the way of the Messiah. The Lord God of Israel is visiting his people with salvation, with redemption. The horn of salvation is rising, and Israel's promised Messiah is coming to rule on the throne of David. The prophets had long foretold of this glorious day—a day when the enemies of God will scatter and their evil grip will be shattered. The mercy of God has dawned as he brings to fruition his holy covenant, the covenant and oath God swore to father Abraham. God's people, delivered from their enemies, will now serve God without fear, in holiness and righteousness all their days.

Zechariah also knew that God had commissioned his son John to give the knowledge of salvation to God's people, to declare the tender mercy of God in Christ, to announce the forgiveness of sins. This was the calling that John fulfilled, even unto death. He came to prepare the way of the Lord, to call sinners to repentance, and to declare that in Christ the promised salvation of God has arrived.

In that sense, Christmas thunders that our task is essentially a continuation of John's. He came to prepare the way, while we preach Jesus, the way, the truth, and the life. But the message is the same. All of God's people across the world join the faithful line of preachers, missionaries, and ministers before them who, like John, gave knowledge of salvation to the people by declaring the tender mercies of God that promise the forgiveness of sins.

That is the mission, the calling, the urgency. The celebration of the birth of Christ puts everything on the table. The unswerving directness and crystalizing simplicity of the Christmas message leave no room for confusion. Reading the Gospel texts, we know we either believe or run away. This is either the greatest truth ever declared, or it is the saddest lie ever told. The Christmas story cannot be reduced to a sentimental tale that gives humanity a warm glow. When the heavenly host declares Jesus is the Savior, Christ the Lord, they announce the forgiveness of sins to those who repent and believe, and they declare war on those who would oppose this child.

In these days, our task is to raise up a generation of faithful, urgent, learned, and skilled counterrevolutionaries for the kingdom of Christ—an insurgency against the principalities and the powers. That is what Zechariah was declaring as John's mission. That is what we declare every year when we celebrate the birth of Christ. Indeed, that should be our anthem every day of every year.

The clarity of the Christmas story reminds us that we must live as defenders of the faith, teachers of undiluted truth, guardians of the treasure entrusted to us, heralds of the gospel of Jesus Christ. God, through the preaching of his Word, has taught us the faith once for all delivered to the saints. God has grounded every one of us in his inspired, inerrant, and infallible Word. Through the ministry of the church, God equips *all* his people for gospel ministry in every facet of life. This he does as a divine mandate to go—go make disciples of all the nations, baptizing them in the name of the Father, and of the Son, and of the Holy Spirit, teaching them to obey all of Christ's commands, knowing that God has promised that his enabling presence will be with us every day (Matt. 28:18–20).

And the source, the fount, the wellspring of our mission began with a baby in a manger, swaddled in a blanket, tended to by his loving mother. There in that manger lay God incarnate. He broke into the world to save it from sin. Now he summons every believer to take the good news and shout it from the mountaintops. Indeed, as Isaiah said, "How beautiful on the mountains are the feet of the herald, who proclaims peace, who brings news of good things, who proclaims salvation, who says to Zion, 'Your God reigns!'" (Isa. 52:7).

Brothers and Sisters in Jesus Christ, the glory of Christmas means so much more than decorated trees, cookies, and presents. Christmas marks the inbreaking of hope, peace, and the salvation of the world. Go now and declare the splendor of this season. Go and proclaim to the world that their King has come, that he paid for their sins, that he died for their redemption, and that eternal life awaits them if they would but believe. This is the glory of Christmas.

For the Fall and Rising of Many in Israel

*Then Simeon blessed them and told his
mother Mary, "Indeed, this child is destined
to cause the fall and rise of many in Israel
and to be a sign that will be opposed, and
a sword will pierce your own soul—that the
thoughts of many hearts may be revealed."*

Luke 2:34–35

I have never received a Christmas card depicting Armageddon. No one has yet sent me a Christmas card that takes war as its theme, picturing Christ as the rider on a white horse, a sword coming from his mouth, ready to rule the nations with a rod of iron. This too, however, is the accomplishment of Christ's messianic mission but one rarely, if ever, mentioned at Christmas. Christmas cards frequently cite the first half of Luke 2. Few, however, draw inspiration from the last half of the chapter.

Simeon was a devout man and was at the temple when Mary and Joseph came for purification according to the law. He lived a long life and experienced the dreadful effects of sin on the world. One thing kept him going: hope in God. He hoped in the Lord and his Anointed. He had a sure confidence that God would be true to his promises and send the Messiah, the one who would deliver Israel from bondage. As Mary and Joseph presented the infant Jesus in the temple, Simeon saw the Lord's salvation at work. He saw Jesus, whom the Father sent into the world to take on human flesh, who would grow up into adulthood, and who "increased in wisdom and stature, and in favor with God and with people" (Luke 2:52). Simeon saw the One who would live the perfect life by obeying God's law completely, thus fulfilling all righteousness, for him. Simeon saw the One who would give himself as a sacrifice to appease the wrath of God. Simeon saw the one who would die so that his sins would be forgiven and he could gain eternal life. In the temple Simeon held salvation in his arms.

God, moreover, spoke through Simeon, and Simeon's prophecy was bracing: "Behold, this child is appointed for the fall and rising of many in Israel" (Luke 2:34 ESV).

You do not often see these verses on a Christmas card. In truth, I have never seen these verses used as a

Christmas inscription. But there it is, right in the heart of the Christmas story.

Simeon told Mary, and Mary directly, that the child to whom she had given birth just days before, the child who had been miraculously conceived within her by the Holy Spirit, was "appointed for the fall and rising of many in Israel."

We know from the numerous prophecies in the Old Testament that Jesus was the long-awaited Messiah. In the first book of the Bible, we find the prophecy that the seed of the woman, Eve, would be at enmity with the seed of the serpent, that is, the devil. In the end, however, the seed of the woman, Jesus Christ, will come and triumph over Satan. Satan and his seed will bruise Christ's heel, but Christ will crush the head of the serpent (Gen. 3:15). The Son of God was appointed by the Father to conquer Satan and death.

Simeon, however, revealed another aspect of Jesus's incarnation. Many nations have and will fall by the hand of Christ, who judges the proud. These nations "rage and the peoples plot in vain[.] The kings of the earth take their stand, and the rulers conspire together against the LORD and his Anointed One: 'Let's tear off their chains and throw their ropes off of us'" (Ps. 2:1–3). They despise God and his commandments and desire to overthrow him. They would rather be the creator instead of being creatures of the Almighty Creator. They sit and plot how to overthrow his kingship. Yet our God "who sits in the heavens laughs; the Lord holds them in derision" (v. 4 ESV). No one, not even the most powerful kingdom on earth, could harm and overthrow our Almighty God. He therefore laughs at their vain attempts.

In response to the vain attempt to overthrow him by these proud and angry kings, our Lord "has done a mighty deed with his arm; he has scattered the proud because of the thoughts of their hearts; he has toppled the mighty from their thrones and exalted the lowly" (Luke 1:51–52). The proud cannot stand before God and live.

Clearly, the response to Jesus—even the baby Jesus— exemplified this pattern. The falling and the rising began immediately, and it was not limited to Israel. That falling and rising has never ceased, and it will cease only when the Lord Christ returns to establish his kingdom in its fullness. Until then, headlines will tell of fallings and ris- ings. From the house of Herod to the Roman Empire, to the Soviet Union, and, inevitably, to the mightiest nations on earth today, we see empires rise and empires fall. From Genesis to Revelation, from the beginning to the end of time, nations will rise and fall, kingdoms will come and go, dominions will appear and disappear—all waiting for God's coming judgment.

But Simeon traced the rise and fall of many in Israel back to the baby laid in Bethlehem's manger. The Lord who is calling out ministers of his gospel and servants of his church is the Lord who will rule the nations and judge them, who reigns and judges even now. He has sounded forth the trumpet that shall never call retreat.

Until he comes, we are witnesses to the fall and rise of many—of kings and empires and dynasties and world orders. And yet all is well with our souls. Why? Because the incarnation of Jesus, and all that we celebrate at Christmas, was the inbreaking of God into a lost and dying world. With the coming of the Son of Man comes the reversal of the curse. With the baby in a manger comes the new epoch in salvation history where Christ is making all things until he returns to set up his eternal kingdom.

This is a triumphant reality Christians can and must celebrate this Christmas. We must see what Simeon proclaimed: that nations will rise and fall because they will ultimately give way to the babe who will not be tamed but forever shall rule.

Far as the Curse Is Found

Christ redeemed us from the curse
of the law by becoming a curse for
us, because it is written, "Cursed is
everyone who is hung on a tree."

Galatians 3:13

We learned earlier in the December 14 reading that one of our favorite Christmas hymns, "Joy to the World," was not originally written for the Advent season. Despite this, it has become a cherished song that millions of Christians sing every year as we celebrate the birth of Christ. The lyrics contain glorious theological truths easily applied to the birth of Jesus.

Isaac Watts wrote "Joy to the World" in 1719. During his life, Watts led in the development of hymns in the English tradition, drawing many of his hymn texts directly from the Psalms. "Joy to the World" was one such hymn, and he based it on Psalm 98, a hymn that declares creation's joy when the Lord comes to rule and to judge. When we sing, "Joy to the world, the Lord is come!" we often think of it applying to Jesus's birth in Bethlehem. It gives us words so we can rejoice in the gift of the incarnate, infant Christ. However, though Watts had Christ's second coming in mind, it must be pointed out that this hymn is not *irrelevant* to the Christmas season, not at all. The song reminds us that Christmas is *not yet over*, for the promises of Christmas are not yet fulfilled, *but they will be*. Earth will fully receive her King. And this King will be received on earth when Christ comes again to reign and to rule, as Psalm 98 promises. Christmas helps us look to Christ's incarnation, which in turn reminds us to look forward to his return.[11]

The third verse of this hymn is what I want to focus on for today's devotion—a lyric with spectacular truths Christians need to praise God for during this Advent season. It reads, "No more let sins and sorrows grow, / nor thorns infest the ground. / He comes to make his blessings flow / far as the curse is found, / far as the curse is found."[12] That is to say the Lord Jesus will make *blessings* abound wherever the curse is currently found. The reversal of the curse is promised in the coming of the Messiah and the fulfillment of his finished, atoning work. Implicit in this third verse also is the promise of the new creation. We live in light of that promise, even as we look back to Bethlehem and celebrate Christmas. When rightly understood, looking back on Christmas helps us look forward to the new creation. The new creation which is to come.

Now carefully consider the reference to the curse in this hymn. Christ's victory over sin is declared to extend "far as the curse is found."[3] When we think about the curse, our minds should immediately think of Genesis 3, where sin and death entered the creation after Adam and Eve broke God's command. The curse began to undo the created order, and it also severed the relationship between God and man. Thus, in Adam, all humanity is born corrupted and depraved; we deserve, by virtue of our sinful nature, eternal punishment for our sins. That is the full measure of the curse. The curse extends to every atom and molecule of creation—from coast to coast, shore to shore, every square inch of the cosmos has succumbed to the curse of sin. All of us have sinned against God. As Paul writes in Romans 3:23, "For all have sinned and fall short of the glory of God."

But God, in unspeakable mercy, made a promise to Adam and Eve in Genesis 3:15 when God condemned the serpent: "I will put hostility between you and the woman, and between your offspring and her offspring. He will strike your head, and you will strike his heel." This was the first promise revealed to mankind: that one day God would make all things new through *a Son*.

That is the background to the line in "Joy to the World." We can sing of joy because the coming of Christ is the fulfillment of that promise. As far as the curse is found, the Messiah has come to undo the curse and to bring the people of God into a restored, eternal relationship with God.

In Galatians 3:10–14, Paul argues that everyone who relies on works of the law remains under the curse. Righteousness and justification before God only come by faith—faith in the perfect, completed work of Jesus Christ. In fact, as Paul writes, "Christ redeemed us from the curse of the law by becoming a curse for us, because it is written, 'Cursed is everyone who is hung on a tree'" (Gal. 3:13). Christ redeemed us from the curse of the law by *becoming* a curse for us—in our stead. What we sinners could not, and cannot, do for ourselves, Christ has done for us already. He removes the curse and the power of the law which condemn us. The curse that reaches throughout every sphere of creation and life more broadly is the precise locale into which the blessing of Christ enters. Therefore, it does not matter—for those in Christ—how far the curse is found because wherever that curse is found, Christ has become such that those who have faith in him would become a blessing.

Though Isaac Watts did not exactly have Christmas in mind when he penned "Joy to the World," it is nonetheless wonderful that his magnificent hymn is sung at Christmas. When the Lord Jesus put on flesh and was born of Mary, this was Joy being brought into the world in a real sense. That night was a marvelous night—a night that caused the angelic choir to sing, "Glory to God in the highest, and on earth peace among those with whom he is pleased!" (Luke 2:14 ESV). This was a birth so glorious that it is still celebrated annually across the globe. And it is no wonder the birth of Jesus brought joy to the world. That baby would one day die as a curse on our behalf, so that those who have faith in him would be blessed.

Joy to the world, indeed, for sin and sorrows are giving way. Jesus has come to make his blessings flow, far as the curse is found—and they do flow.

Do We Really Believe What We Say We Believe?

The Word became flesh and dwelt
among us. We observed his glory, the
glory as the one and only Son from
the Father, full of grace and truth.

John 1:14

Anglican theologian and author Harry Blamires wrote something that made a significant impact on me as a college student. It was a book about the life of the Christian mind, and he argued, "There is no longer a Christian mind. It is commonplace that the mind of modern man has been secularized. . . . It has been deprived of any orientation towards the supernatural. Tragic as this fact is, it would not be so desperately tragic had the Christian mind held out against the secular drift."[14]

He lamented an enormous problem regarding the mind of even evangelical Christians in an increasingly secular age. We become too easily conditioned by our cultural context. The secular and common replace the supernatural and glorious.

God, however, commands us to resist this drift. Taking care of our minds so that we see, savor, and revel in the glory of God is a crucial matter for Christian discipleship, especially in our post-Christian age. God means for those made in his image to know and engage him. Indeed, Isaiah speaks of this intention when he declares, "You will keep the mind that is dependent on you in perfect peace, for it is trusting in you" (Isa. 26:3). We all long for peace, and Isaiah explains that peace of a perfect, unceasing quality comes to the one who properly orients his or her mind on the things of God. Paul, moreover, told the Christians at Rome that they must endeavor not to be conformed to the pattern of this world but to be transformed by the renewal of their minds (Rom. 12:2). The same is true for us.

Surrendering the supernatural to the secular can happen at Christmas. Christians too have a particular temptation to let this season pass by as a commercialized, secular holiday manufactured by our culture. We must resist this temptation and reflect on the truths without which this season would not exist. We need to ask ourselves the question, "Do we believe what we believe we believe?" In other words, if we understand the central teachings of Christianity and say we believe them, do our beliefs move us in such a way that confirms we really believe them? Do our beliefs actually influence our lives? Do we live as a people who truly believe that the Word became flesh? If he did, then it changes everything, and we had better live like it.

Our integrity as disciples of Jesus Christ depends on our ability to look inwardly and ask ourselves what we believe and how—or if—those beliefs grip our affections. Verbal and intellectual assent is easy; it is another thing altogether to be transformed by what we say we believe.

When John wrote, "The Word became flesh and dwelt among us. We observed his glory, the glory as the one and only Son from the Father, full of grace and truth" (John 1:14), he declared a life-changing, cosmos-altering truth Christians say we celebrate at Christmas. If you let the secularized Christmas holiday drown out this truth, you will never see the glory of Christmas for what it is; you will stumble through this season, robbed of the spectacular truths God wants you to savor.

If the Word has indeed become flesh and dwelt among us, it does change everything. We can face all the headlines of this age. We can faithfully endure whatever this world will throw at the church. We can face the past, traverse the present, and hope for the future. We can face time and eternity because of the great truth of what it means that the Word became flesh; but if it's not true, we are lost. We are dead in our sin. We have no hope. But Jesus came and everything has changed.

Christian, the Word indeed became flesh. Believe it and live like you believe it. Don't let this season pass you by without letting the truth that God's Son came into the world to save you fill you with an unconquerable joy. We celebrate Christmas because we believe in the truth of the gospel of Jesus Christ. We believe every single biblical claim of the Christmas story. All of it was a fulfillment of God's promises, and everything recorded—all the supernatural beauty of God breaking into the world—should steady our minds and nourish our souls.

Everything about the Christmas story is true, and it all points to why Jesus came. In fact, read John 1:14 together with John 3:16: "We observed his glory, the glory as the one and only Son from the Father, full of grace and truth. . . . For God loved the world in this way: He gave his one and only Son, so that everyone who believes in him will not perish but have eternal life." We believe and celebrate at Christmas the most important truth anyone could hear and know: God the Father sent God the Son to save sinners because God so loved the world that he willingly gave up his Son for us.

We know this is true, and we must *truly* believe it. We cannot let our Christian minds succumb to the secular.

God wants far more for us than a commercialized season; he wants us to experience the fullness of joy that comes by receiving and worshipping the Word made flesh.

The Light of Christmas

The people walking darkness have seen
a great light; a light has dawned on
those living in the land of darkness.

Isaiah 9:2

Those words from the prophet Isaiah told of the coming Prince of Peace and of the light and life he would bring.

Christmas arrives again with all the promise of remembrance and celebration. Christians celebrate Christmas because the light did dawn. The birth of Jesus in Bethlehem was not only the fulfillment of biblical prophecy, but the dawn of a new age. As the angels declared to the shepherds, this infant is "a Savior, who is Christ the Lord" (Luke 2:11 ESV).

This is the essence of Christmas: the birth of the Savior. To understand Christmas is to know that the ultimate peace the Savior would bring would be established by his death and resurrection. Even as Jesus came to save his people from their sins, Christ's birth points toward his cross and the fulfillment of his saving work.

When Isaiah told of the coming Prince of Peace, he spoke of light dispelling darkness. The metaphor of light is central to our celebration of Christmas. After all, even as John introduces his Gospel by identifying Jesus as the Word who became flesh, John also describes Jesus as "the true light that gives light to everyone was coming into the world" (John 1:9).

The image of light dispelling darkness is central to our understanding of the incarnation and its meaning. When Jesus was presented at the temple shortly after his birth, the aged Simeon recognized this child as "a light for revelation to the Gentiles, and glory to your people Israel" (Luke 2:32).

The metaphor of light makes sense only against a background of darkness. In the Bible, darkness is a rich metaphor that points to a double reality. In one sense, darkness points to the simple fact of human ignorance. Those who are "in the dark" are those who lack knowledge. To the Jewish mind, this metaphor had particular application to the Gentile world—a world that had not received the grace of God through the revelation of the Torah, the prophets, and the written revelation of God. Even today, we know that untold millions still dwell in deep darkness, having never heard about the one true God or of Jesus Christ, his only Son.

In a second sense, darkness refers to evil and willful blindness. This points beyond the mere fact of simple ignorance. In this sense, darkness refers to the fact that many will *reject* the light. As John explained, "He was in the world, and the world was created through him, and yet the world did not recognize him. He came to his own, and his own people did not receive Him" (John 1:10–11).

This is hard to believe. The Son of God took on human flesh and came to live among sinful humanity, but the vast majority did not recognize him for who he is.

As a celebration of light, Christmas is the festival that points to the glory of God in the revelation of the Son in Bethlehem's humble manger. We rightly point to Christ's birth as the central event of human history—the dividing line between the age of darkness and the age of light. This is reason enough to celebrate Christmas, for our response to this gift of light must be a celebration, thanksgiving, and rejoicing.

Preaching on a Christmas morning almost five hundred years ago, Martin Luther reminded his congregation that the proper response to the Christian story is not mere rejoicing or casual interest but *faith*. Beyond this, Luther understood that this faith has two important dimensions.

Luther argued that most persons know how to rejoice when they are given a Christmas gift. "But how many are there who shout and jump for joy when they hear the message of the angel: 'To you is born this day the Savior?' Indeed, the majority look upon it as a sermon that must be preached, and when they have heard it, consider it a trifling thing, and go away just as they were before. This shows that we have neither the first nor the second faith."[15]

As Luther understood, to hear the Christmas story and respond with mere interest is an indication of faith's absence. Furthermore, Luther helpfully reminded his congregation that a mere affirmation of the fact that the incarnation occurred is not saving faith. "We do not believe that the virgin mother bore a son and that he is the Lord and Savior unless, added to this, I believe the second thing, namely, that he is my Savior and Lord."[16]

In other words, the message of Christmas is received when Jesus Christ is not merely affirmed as the baby in Bethlehem's manger but as one's own Savior and Lord.

"When I can say: This I accept as my own, because the angel meant it for me, then, if I believe it in my heart, I shall not fail to love the mother Mary, and even more the child, and especially the Father," Luther continued. "For, if it is true that the child was born of the virgin and is mine, then I have no angry God and I must know and feel that there is nothing but laughter and joy in the heart of the Father and no sadness in my heart. For, if what the angel says is true, that he is our Lord and Savior, what can sin do against us?"[17]

With those words, Luther articulated the majestic faith of Christmas—the faith that saves. When Christmas is rightly understood, we know that God loves us, even as we are sinners who deserve no love. We also understand that this love is demonstrated in the gift of the Son, who would die for our sins and would be raised by the Father in order to secure our salvation.

Thus, a true Christmas is celebrated when we come to understand, to know, to celebrate, and to receive the fact that Jesus Christ is not merely a Savior but *our* Savior—even *my* Savior and *your* Savior.

The image of light is central not only to Christmas but to Christianity. Jesus said: "I am the light of the world. Anyone who follows me will never walk in the darkness but will have the light of life" (John 8:12). This is the sum and substance of Christmas. The people who walked in darkness have seen a great light. Those who lived in a dark land now experience the shining of the Light of life.

Born that Man No More May Die

For God loved the world in this way:
He gave his one and only Son, so that
everyone who believes in him will
not perish but have eternal life.
John 3:16

To be human is to be immersed in life and its affairs. Work and worries are never far from reach, and they threaten to interrupt without notice or apology. Even as families gather for Christmas, someone still works most newsrooms, the military remains on alert, and medical personnel continue their works of mercy. Furthermore, someone is probably hard at work in the kitchen.

The celebration of Christmas is always a bit awkward for Christians. Unbelievers can simply latch on to Christmas as a holiday. Believers know that *every* day is a celebration of the birth, life, death, and resurrection of the

Lord Jesus Christ. We do not believe or preach anything at Christmas that Christians have not believed and preached every day of every year since Jesus established his church.

Some Christians worry that Christmas has been so corrupted by consumerism and triviality that it cannot be rescued from confusion. And yet Christians need the annual celebrations of the birth and resurrection of Jesus Christ. We need the annual affirmations of the incarnation of the Son of God and his resurrection from the dead. We need the truth proclaimed and the joy expressed. We need the festivals as we live out the faith. We need the carols and the candles and the bells. We need the wonder on the faces of our children and the glory on the faces of the old. We need the great Christmas hymns, and we need to sing them. We need little children dressed like shepherds and miniature wise men from the east.

The devil hates all true Christmas carols, but there are particular carols with specific words that must infuriate him beyond measure. Just consider these words from "Hark! The Herald Angels Sing": "Mild he lays his glory by, born that we no more may die, born to raise us from the earth, born to give us second birth."[18]

In terms of pedigree and poetry, it is hard to match "Hark! The Herald Angels Sing" in the evangelical heritage. The words were originally composed by Charles Wesley in 1739. Charles was the great hymn writer and companion to his brother, John Wesley, the great evangelist. Rivaling the sixteenth-century reformers in influence, the Wesleys transformed evangelical Christianity. John's words started an entire movement and brought many to Christ. Charles's words are sung every week, hymn after hymn, in evangelical churches.

But nearly twenty years after Charles Wesley wrote the hymn, another father of evangelical Christianity slightly modified it and made it even more popular in the churches. George Whitefield taught more Christians to declare the truth of Christmas through this hymn and shortened it so that the gospel content would be even more clear. Christ was "born that we no more may die, born to raise us from the earth, born to give us second birth."[9]

Jesus made the second birth so clear when he spoke to Nicodemus as recorded in John 3. Jesus was born in Bethlehem so that he might die for our sins, raise us to glory, and give us a second birth. Salvation and the new birth come to sinners who believe in Jesus Christ, repent of sins, and trust in Christ alone.

Jesus was born that men no more may die. The gospel promises everlasting life to all who believe in him. Jesus saves.

A few chapters ago I mentioned one of my favorite Christmas traditions, the annual "Service of Nine Lessons and Carols" at King's College Chapel, Cambridge. The most familiar of the services was arranged by the late Sir David Willcocks, who chose "Hark! The Herald Angels Sing" as the recessional hymn for the service. The choir and congregation conclude worship with the hymn, introduced and concluded with magnificent trumpet fanfares. Thus, the service ends with the stanza including the words "born that we no more may die." Then: "Hark! The herald angels sing, Glory to the newborn king."[20]

Praise to the triune God—Father, Son, and Holy Spirit—for our salvation.

The troubling headlines will wait. The contentious issues will beckon again. But, for now, revel in Christmas and in the incarnation of Christ the Lord. Share a meal, hug your loved ones, kiss a grandchild's precious face, and sing a hymn.

Glory to the newborn king.

In the Fullness of Time

But when the fullness of time had come, God sent forth his Son, born of woman, born under the law, to redeem those who were under the law, so that we might receive adoption as sons.

Galatians 4:4–5 ESV

In Galatians 4, Paul begins discussing different forms of spiritual bondage. In particular, Paul addressed members within the Galatian church who had returned to a form of legalism that sprang from the teachings of the Judaizers. The law of God did not promote legalism. On the contrary, the law distills the exact type of obedience and worship that pleases the Lord—a contrite obedience clothed with faith in the promises of God.

Verse 4, however, shifts the argument. Paul writes, "But when the *fullness* of time had come, God sent forth his Son, born of woman, born under the law, to redeem those who were under the law, so that we might receive adoption as sons" (Gal. 4:4–5 ESV, emphasis added). The word used for "fullness" refers to the readiness, presence, and provision of all things. It also means "greatness," as in full authority and majesty. Thus, when the fullness of time came, God sent forth his Son.

This verse, therefore, situates the coming of Christ in a historical context. The incarnation *happened* at a point in time, at a point in history. The whole world changed with the incarnation. Even the calendar bears the impact of Christ's incarnation. When you write the date, you include a year that stretches back to the birth of the eternal Son of God.

The historicity of the incarnation possesses tremendous significance for the Christmas season. When believers talk about the Christmas story, their discussion does not center on a myth or a legend. The Christmas story makes a historical claim—a direct, honest, unhesitant conviction that the things recorded in Scripture *actually happened* just as God revealed them. The Advent of Christ occurred in space *and* in time. Indeed, the incarnation flowed from a stream of prophecies that looked forward to the day when the Messiah would come. Christmas, therefore, means more than another day to mark off the calendar. It was a day the prophets ached for fruition—a day when God would come to set his people free from the bondage of sin.

Paul's declaration that the incarnation marked the fullness of time raises an important question: Why then? Why was it the fullness of time? Why in the reign of Caesar Augustus did Christ's birth take place?

There were certainly important historical realities at the time of Christ's incarnation that were conducive to the dissemination of the gospel and the growth of the early church. Indeed, the sovereign providence of God willed for Jesus's ministry to take place at the perfect time, in the perfect place, in the perfect circumstances and context.

Still, the fact that God made for a unique moment in human history cannot be the totality of what Paul meant in Galatians 4. The "fullness of time" Paul had in mind extends far beyond the historical context of Jesus's incarnation. In Galatians 4, Paul links the theme of fullness of time with the bondage of man to the law:

> I mean that the heir, as long as he is a
> child, is no different from a slave, though
> he is the owner of everything, but he is
> under guardians and managers until the
> date set by his father. In the same way
> we also, when we were children, were

> enslaved to the elementary principles
> of the world. But when the fullness of
> time had come, God sent forth his Son,
> born of a woman, born under the law, to
> redeem those who were under the law, so
> that we might receive adoption as sons.
> And because you are sons, God has sent
> the Spirit of his Son into our hearts, cry-
> ing, "Abba! Father!" So you are no longer
> a slave, but a son, and if a son, then an
> heir through God. (Gal. 4:1–7 ESV)

Paul believed that even the Hebrew people, God's covenant people, should have sensed a reality of spiritual desperation in the law. God's perfect law demanded perfect obedience. The nation of Israel had failed, time and again, to live up to its covenant obligations. The law continu- ally pointed the people toward sacrifices that would make atonement for their sin—sacrifices performed continually because they could not affect eternal atonement. Indeed, no amount of sacrifices could alter the hearts of the people. The people remained—year after year, century after cen- tury—under the curse of the law and the curse of sin.

The predicament of man's depravity, however, extends to all humanity, Jew and Gentile alike. Thus, through- out Israel's history, prophets appeared and proclaimed a glorious anticipation. They longed for, preached about, and announced a day when God would intervene. Only an act of divine mercy and power could rescue Israel—indeed, the whole cosmos—from the ravages of sin. The fall of Adam and Eve plunged all creation into the mire of sin and death. All mankind lived in an inescapable slavery to Satan and death. Humanity had no alternative course but eternal perdition. There was no escape save an act of God's mercy.

That mercy came, in the fullness of time, through Jesus Christ, "born of a woman, born under the law" (Gal. 4:4). These two phrases thunder with Christological glory and pronounce the gracious intervention of God, which the church celebrates at Christmas. First, by declaring that the Son was "born of a woman," Paul espoused the full humanity of Jesus, the Son of God. In the fullness of time, God himself intervened on behalf of his people. Redemption, however, must work through man, for man rightly stood condemned. The wrath of God must be poured out on sin, and the only sufficient mediator between God and man could only have been the incarnate God: Christ the Son of God *and* the Son of Man.

Second, Jesus was born "under the law." While mankind lived under the curse of the law, the God-man had come to break the shackles of man's slavery. Jesus Christ, by nature of his birth, lived under the full weight of the law's demands. He, furthermore, lived *perfectly*, meeting

123

every command of the law with unwavering obedience. Indeed, Jesus not only obeyed the law, but he became the perfect sacrifice required by the law. The blood of goats and sheep under the old covenant could never enact a lasting atonement. The blood of the spotless Lamb, however, *could* fulfill the law's demands. In the fullness of time, Jesus Christ obeyed the law and became our sacrifice. This he did not only to redeem God's people but to secure for them an eternal adoption as children of the King.

Your adoption as sons and daughters should fill your time of worship this Christmas season. Jesus's incarnation meant that he came, not as a distant Messiah and Savior, but as one of us—one who was "the firstborn among many brothers" (Rom. 8:29 ESV). The salvation secured through Christ not only pays the price of sin, but it also guarantees a glorious inheritance by making sinners into saints, rebels into redeemed sons and daughters. Indeed, the gospel promises *adoption* for all who have faith in Christ. The power of the gospel does not merely free you from sin; it makes you a child of the living God: "For you did not receive the spirit of slavery to fall back into fear, but you have received the Spirit of adoption as sons, by whom we cry, 'Abba! Father!'" (Rom. 8:15 ESV).

The Christmas story stands in the line of Israel's history. Christmas is an anticipated event, not a historical accident. Indeed, the incarnation, at the fullness of time, was God's divine act of mercy. He broke *into* history to redeem the whole world from the curse of the law wherein all stand condemned to suffer the full wrath of God's justice. A historical event two thousand years ago became the fulcrum of human history and the Christian faith. In the fullness of time, God broke through the history of sin and rebellion and redeemed his people through the incarnate Son.

23

Christ, Our Salvation

*This saying is trustworthy and
deserving of full acceptance: "Christ
Jesus came into the world to save
sinners"—and I am the worst of them.*

1 Timothy 1:15

B ehind the call of every Christian, whether those engaged in full-time ministry or the multitude serving faithfully as lay members of churches, there is a testimony of God's saving work. The gospel serves as the foundation for all our lives and becomes the single most important event during our earthly pilgrimage.

Christmas, moreover, affords us the opportunity to reflect on and worship God for his saving grace. In fact, we dare not miss the entire reason for this magnificent season. Amid the commercialization and secularized temptations that lure us away from the glory of Christmas, do not miss what the apostle Paul told Timothy about the mission of Jesus's incarnation: "This saying is trustworthy and deserving of full acceptance: 'Christ Jesus came into the world to save sinners'—and I am the worst of them" (1 Tim. 1:15).

Christ came into the world to save sinners! The majesty of Christmas, and what makes this season truly joyful, hinges on the reason for Jesus's incarnation. The only reason the gospel is the good news of salvation is precisely because Christ has come, born of the virgin, to live the sinless life and pay the ultimate price for our sins. The baby in the manger was there to begin the work of reversing the curse and to wash his people white with his blood.

The most trustworthy statement we will ever know is that Christ Jesus came into the world to save sinners. Whatever you face this season—the loss of loved ones, the busyness of life, financial hardship, wayward children, a distant spouse—Christmas comes as a time to know and experience the triumphant hope that Christ has come to save you. He has come to bring peace between you and God. Indeed, this is far more than the reason for the season. That Christ came to save sinners is the only reason we have hope. As Paul wrote in Romans 5:8, "While we were still sinners, Christ died for us."

The babe of Bethlehem is none other than the Savior of the world—the one for whom God so loved the world and gave his only Son. Indeed, "for God did not send his Son into the world to condemn the world, but to save the world through him" (John 3:17).

This glorious news, moreover, must be situated as Paul understood it in his letter to Timothy. Paul stated, "This saying is trustworthy and deserving of full acceptance: 'Christ Jesus came into the world to save sinners'—and *I am the worst of them*" (1 Tim. 1:15, emphasis added). This was more than a theoretical knowledge of sin; Paul knew himself as a sinner in need of salvation.

Christmas must be a time to remember that, except for the incarnation, we would be lost in sin. Remembering our sin and our depravity as a devotional exercise at Christmas should not devolve into self-degradation and heaping shame on ourselves. On the contrary, we magnify the joy of this season when we remember that we were dead in our trespasses and sins and were, by nature, children of wrath like the rest of mankind (Eph. 2:3). We must take up this season as an opportunity to recount our need for salvation and to celebrate that God sent his Son to redeem us from the kingdom of darkness. Jesus saves!

What greater gift could we imagine at a time of year when the giving of gifts is customary and proper? What greater gift can we share with others or tell our family members than this glorious truth: we were all doomed for an eternity in hell, but thanks be to God who sent Christ Jesus into the world to save sinners.

Do you want to recapture the glory of Christmas? Then, with Paul, remember where you would be apart from the incarnation. Out of that knowledge, let the love of God in Christ for you nourish your faith, deepen your hope, and fill you with nothing less than adoration and worship. Christmas fills the Christian heart with astounding joy. Don't resist it.

24

The Babe Who Will Not Be Tamed

In these last days, he has spoken to us by
his Son. God has appointed him heir of all
things and made the universe through him.

Hebrews 1:2

The annual Festival of the Incarnation, commonly known as Christmas, comes to the commercial world as a financial windfall, but it comes to the church as a summons. Substituting the truth of God for a lie, the secular world cannot but confuse the manger with Santa's sleigh or the shepherds with elves. We should not be surprised by the commercialization of Christmas; it is the natural reflex of a fallen world in unbelief.

But Christians know that Christmas is not really a holiday or a season. Indeed, Christmas comes as a call to faith and witness. Only those who know Christ know what

Christmas is all about, and the church will respond with either faith or faithlessness.

The real issue at Christmas is the identity of the Child in the manger. If the babe is merely one who grew to serve as a great moral teacher, a founder of a major world religion, an example of service and humility, then the world can handle him quite comfortably.

If the child, however, lived and breathed as the incarnate Son of God—he who came as "Word of the Father, now in flesh appearing"[21]—the world has a major problem. When the church presents the manger as a mere sentimental object lesson of divine love, the world smiles and moves on. But when the church speaks the truth—that the child of the manger is the God who comes as both judgment *and* grace— the world sees the infant as a truth it must attempt to tame.

Christmas, therefore, is first a call to faith—a call to look in the manger and see God in human flesh. The writer of the Epistle to the Hebrews understood this well. He wrote, "Long ago, at many times and in many ways, God spoke to our fathers by the prophets, but in these last days he has spoken to us by his Son, whom he appointed the heir of all things, through whom also he created the world" (Heb. 1:1–2 ESV).

There in that manger in Bethlehem lay the fully human, fully divine Son of the eternal God. The creation longed for his coming. The prophets proclaimed his reign.

Then Mary held him in her arms. The fullness of God's revelation broke into the world as a humble infant.

This is the babe who cannot be tamed. The book of Hebrews states that this "Son is the radiance of God's glory and the exact expression of his nature, sustaining all things by his powerful word" (Heb. 1:3). This babe, therefore, is the One who was God in human flesh, the divine God-man who had been promised by the Father through the prophets of old and was born of a virgin in Bethlehem. But the babe in the manger must never be separated from the Jesus who cleansed the temple, performed mighty miracles, and claimed, "I am the way, the truth, and the life. No one comes to the Father except through me" (John 14:6).

The manger led to a cross, where Christ died as our substitute, bearing our sins and, as Hebrews states, making purification for our sins (Heb. 1:3). The divine babe of the manger is the one who would die on a cross and, on the third day, rise from the grave. Christmas aims at Good Friday and Resurrection Sunday. The unfathomable truth of Christmas is that this babe was born to die—and to die for sinners.

This means Christmas can never be trivialized or sentimentalized by the church. The babe is tender, gentle, and meek; but he is also the One who holds all things together by the power of his word (Heb. 1:3) and will judge both the quick and the dead (1 Pet. 4:5). His name is the only name under heaven and earth whereby we must be saved (Acts 4:12).

The church must repent of assisting the world in the evasion of Christmas and speak boldly the truth it knows—the whole, glorious, and offensive truth. The church's role is to preach Christ and bear witness to him, to make certain that when we say "Christmas" the world knows we speak a word of truth.

Christianity stands or falls on this central truth, that God was in Christ reconciling the world to himself. This truth claim makes Christianity Christian and makes it the enemy of unbelief. The Christian faith rests on the twin pillars of the person *and* work of Christ, that is, who Christ is and what he accomplished through his incarnation, death, and resurrection. An attack on one of these truths is an assault on the other. The Christmas truth tells both parts of this story: *The Child who came is the Messiah who saves.* He is also the Lord who reigns.

This means a word of witness. Christmas affords the church an unusual opportunity to tell the world the true identity of the infant of Bethlehem—to share the good news that this babe came to die that we might have life and have it more abundantly (John 10:10).

The world is vulnerable at Christmas. All the commercialization and trivialization of Christmas are but the unbelieving world's defense mechanisms at work. These defenses can be undone by the truth, and the truth is ours to tell. Tell the world the Christmas story—the real Christmas story—of the Babe who will not be tamed. This is the babe we adore.

25

Joy to the World—
Even So Lord,
Come Quickly

Adopt the same attitude as that of Christ Jesus,
who, existing in the form of God, did not consider
equality with God as something to be exploited.
Instead he emptied himself by assuming the form of
a servant, taking on the likeness of humanity. And
when he had come as a man, he humbled himself
by becoming obedient to the point of death—even
to death on a cross. For this reason God highly
exalted him and gave him the name that is above
every name, so that at the name of Jesus every knee
will bow—in heaven and on earth and under the
earth—and every tongue will confess that Jesus
Christ is Lord, to the glory of God the Father.

Philippians 2:5–11

Recapturing the Glory of Christmas

oday, we celebrate the birth of our Savior. Throughout this devotional, I hope the Lord has used his Word to rekindle in you a view of Christmas that truly fills you with joy. I hope you have recaptured the glory of Christmas amid an age and a culture that have so secularized this season that even Christians can forget why we gather with family, wrap presents, and travel hundreds of miles. Today, I hope you worship God for what he has done by sending Christ Jesus into the world and marvel at the truths of the incarnation of the Son. Nothing about this season makes sense, and there is no reason to express joy and hope without the Light coming into the world to save sinners. Whatever you do today, do not let the exceeding wonder of God's mercy and love for you pass you by.

As one final devotional thought, however, I want us to be reminded that while Jesus has indeed come, we long for his second coming. Indeed, Christians throughout the last two millennia have prayed, "Come, Lord Jesus!" (Rev. 22:20). The church has uttered that prayer because the Lord did come; that is why the truth of the incarnation of the Lord Jesus Christ remains the only source for hope. For this reason alone, Christians do not surrender to paranoia or despair, even as we look at devastating headlines or endure constant reminders of sin's continued existence. We know that Christ has come and he sits upon his throne. The hope of our salvation is exactly what we celebrate at

Christmas when we declare for our souls—and for all the world—the incarnation of the Lord Jesus Christ.

Yet our worship during this season is inherently eschatological; it points to something not yet realized. In fact, the Christmas hymn "Joy to the World" includes a stanza that reminds us of the already-but-not-yet realities of Christ's kingdom. If we reflect on the song's meaning, we realize that when we talk about Bethlehem and rejoice in the infant Christ, we do so knowing that Christmas isn't the final word—the promises of Christmas *are not yet fulfilled*. The hymn reads, "No more let sins and sorrows grow, / nor thorns infest the ground. / He comes to make his blessings flow, / far as the curse is found, / far as, far as the curse is found."[22]

The reversal of the curse is promised in the coming of the Messiah and the fulfillment of his atoning work. Implicit in this verse is the promise of new creation. We live in light of that promise, and we long for the day when Christ will return. Indeed, Paul's Christological declaration in Philippians 2:5–11 includes the celebratory, worshipful truths we sing about at Christmas, as well as the longing for Christ to return. The Son of God who was born of the virgin, who took on flesh, and who came to rescue us from our sins is the same Son of God for whom we await. We await the day when sin will be no more and for the day when the entire cosmos will declare what we proclaim at Christmas: "Jesus is Lord!"

The final verse of the hymn "Joy to the World" resounds with that eschatological hope and breathtaking promise: "He rules the world with truth and grace, / and makes the nations prove / the glories of His righteousness / and wonders of His love, / and wonders of His love, / and wonders, and wonders of His love."[23] Those words resound with final, ultimate victory over sin and death. The babe born in Bethlehem—the promised Messiah, the eternal King on David's throne—is the same Son of God who will rule the nations with truth and grace. This is what we pray to see, and this is what we hope for at Christmas. Joy to the world, indeed.

Even so Lord, come quickly.

Merry Christmas to you and yours.

About the Author

R. Albert Mohler Jr. is the president of the Southern Baptist Theological Seminary. He is an esteemed authority on contemporary issues and has been recognized by such influential publications as *Time* and *Christianity Today* as leader among American evangelicals. In addition to his presidential duties, he is a professor of Christian theology and hosts two programs: *The Briefing*, a daily analysis of news and events from a Christian worldview, and *Thinking in Public* a series of conversations with the day's leading thinkers. He is also the editor of *WORLD Opinions* and has authored numerous books, his most recent being *The Conviction to Lead, Revised and Updated Edition: 25 Principles for Leadership That Matters*; *Tell Me the Stories of Jesus: The Explosive Power of Jesus' Parables*; *The Gathering Storm: Secularism, Culture, and the Church*; *The Apostles Creed: Discovering Authentic Christianity in an Age of Counterfeit; The Prayer That Turns the World Upside Down*, and a two-volume commentary on the book of Acts. He served as the general editor of the *Grace and Truth Study Bible*. He also writes a popular blog and a regular commentary on moral, cultural, and theological issues. He loves to celebrate Christmas with his wife, Mary, his son Christopher, and his daughter Katie and son-in-law Riley, along with their three kids: Benjamin, Henry, and Margaret.

Notes

1. Martin Luther, "From Heaven High I Come to You," 1535. Translated by Catherine Winkworth, 1855. From Tinity Hymnal, Revised Edition (Norcross, GA: Great Commission Publications, 1990).

2. Ralph Waldo Emerson, "Divinity School Address," Cambridge, MA, July 15, 1838, https://archive.vcu.edu/english/engweb/transcendentalism/authors/emerson/essays/dsa.html.

3. Emerson, "Divinity School Address."

4. W. Chatterton Dix, "As with Gladness Men of Old," 1858. Public domain.

5. Nicholas D. Kristof, "Believe It, or Not," *New York Times*, August 15, 2003, https://www.nytimes.com/2003/08/15/opinion/believe-it-or-not.html.

6. Thomas Jefferson, "From Thomas Jefferson to John Adams, 11 April 1823," Founders Online, National Archives, accessed March 4, 2024, https://founders.archives.gov/documents/Jefferson/98-01-02-3446.

7. See A. T. Robertson, *The Mother of Jesus: Her Problems and Her Glory* (New York: George H. Doran, 1925).

8. "1918: A Festival of Nine Lessons and Carols," The Recordings of King's College Cambridge, accessed March 4, 2024, https://www.kingscollegerecordings.com/1918-a-festival-of-nine-lessons-and-carols/?v=7516fd43adaa.

9. "1918: A Festival of Nine Lessons and Carols."

10. "1918: A Festival of Nine Lessons and Carols."

11. Isaac Watts, "Joy to the World," 1719. Public domain.

12. Watts, "Joy to the World."

13. Watts, "Joy to the World."

14. Harry Blamires, *The Christian Mind: How Should a Christian Think?* (Ann Arbor, MI: Vine Books, 1997), 3.

15. Martin Luther, "Sermon on the Afternoon of Christmas Day (1530)," from *Martin Luther's Basic Theological Writings*, 3rd edition. Edited by William R. Russel (Mineapolis, MN: Fortress Press, 2012), 174.

16. Luther, "Sermon on the Afternoon of Christmas Day (1530)."

17. Luther, "Sermon on the Afternoon of Christmas Day (1530)."

18. Charles Wesley, "Hark! The Herald Angels Sing," altered by George Whitefield, 1753. Public domain.

19. Wesley, "Hark! The Herald Angels Sing."

20. See December 13th. "1918: A Festival of Nine Lessons and Carols," The Recordings of King's College Cambridge, accessed March 4, 2024, https://www.kingscollegerecordings.com/1918-a-festival-of-nine-lessons-and-carols/?v=7516fd43adaa.

21. John F. Wade, "O Come All Ye Faithful," 1743. Public domain.

22. Watts, "Joy to the World."

23. Watts, "Joy to the World."